THE LITERARY SEMANTICS

OF

KĀLIDĀSA

THE LITERARY SEMANTICS OF KĀLIDĀSA

(A Pragmatic Approach)

H. L. SHUKLA

Gian Publishing House

29/6 SHAKTI NAGAR • DELHI-110007 • INDIA

GIAN PUBLISHING HOUSE
29/6 Shakti Nagar, Delhi-110007

ISBN 81-212-0059-8

Printed in India

Published by Mrs. Gayatri Garg for GianPublishing House, Delhi and Printed at Gupta Printers, E-2/16 Shastri Nagar, Delhi-110052.

PROLOGUE

The Himalayas are our national mountain ; the Ganges is our national river ; the Gītā is our national scripture ; and Kālidāsa is our national poet. There is no appropriate author other than Kālidāsa to be counted as the first. He is probably the first in chronological order and is so in eminence as a poet. He was recognised as the greatest poet by poets and writers of the future generations. There are statements about him that when Kālidāsa is counted as the first among poets, there is no one to be counted as the second to follow him. He is placed with VedaVyāsa, the author of the Mahābhārata, and Vālmīki, the author of the Rāmāyaṇa. They form a trio.

Kālidāsa owes his fame to a number of factors. He is the oldest of the classical poets preserved in the school—tradition of Sanskrit. For centuries, his works Raghuvaṁsha, Kumārasaṁbhava, and Meghadūta inspired Indian children to learn Sanskrit language and poetry.

These poems were taught by school-teachers verse by verse, explaining the formation of each word, furnishing the appropriate rule for each reconstruction, and defining each figure of speech. We have in manuscript-form the lectures of some fifty of these school-teachers from the 10th century A.D. down to the present. That Kālidāsa's poetry could survive such treatment is evidence of the author's invulnerable genius. For these children loved what they memorized and imitated Kālidāsa when they came to write poetry of their own.

Again Kālidāsa is the only author of the classical tradition who wrote plays as well as poems. Other classical authors specialized in one or the other form of writing. The plays, until recently did not form part of the school tradition ; no ancient commentary on them is preserved. They were works that were read privately for pleasure or staged at courts and temples for a selected gathering which accounts for several textual variations. We have three plays of Kālidāsa, which for 1500 years have furnished us with models for aesthetic enjoyment, laughter, love and compassion.

The merits of Kālidāsa's works cannot be gainsaid. Nor do they put all other Indian authors into shade because Sanskrit is too traditional and anti-individualistic medium to produce a concentration of all of its genius in a single man as English did in Shakespeare's case. Kālidāsa's merit is rather a merit of balance: he combines convention and originality, reason and emotion, worldly values and mystical ones, with invariable taste. One can find each of these elements expressed separately in other Sanskrit authors. But no other Sanskrit author keeps the various strands of literature, the various goals of human life in such perfect harmony as Kālidāsa.

Several years have elapsed of the first edition of my book "A Comprehensive Dictionary of Kālidāsa" (Allahabad 1980). Much has transpired.

Writings in the first edition of the '*Dictionary*' pointed to the need to develop a pragmatic approach in our conceptualization, research and practice. Only rarely was such an approach actually adopted. As an extension of this viewpoint, the present book gives very short account of a research programme in progress. The programme has started as an investigation of interpretation, a deeply problematic field of literary semantics.

Although we are not yet to analyze the literary text of Kālidāsa into its most minute constituents, we are beginning to understand of the process of aesthetic-sign-production and sign-processing to attempt a clarification of some notions related to information theory and word-count mathematics, pragmatics, stylistics and non-verbal communication of Kālidāsa.

In this work we deal with some of the burning questions posed by literature in our time. We have laid special stress on the part played by Kālidāsa in the literary process and his relationship with to the intellectual life of society.

While underlining the significance of socialist realism in this book, we have explored it both as an artistic method and as a trend demonstrating the wealth of its artistic potential.

The book provides an analysis of the component elements of poetic style, its aesthetic significance and its social function.

We have explained here the progressive development of literature and art and criticised those theories which deny the existence of artistic progress in Kālidāsa.

HIRA LAL SHUKLA

CONTENTS

1

INTRODUCTION

1.1. The Life and Times of Kālidāsa

To every student of Sanskrit literature, it is a matter of keen regret that neither the poet nor Indian tradition should preserve any authentic information about him. Even a cursory study of his works creates a curiosity in the mind about the author and automatically raises the questions about his life, his parentage, his native place, his patrons and friends, the dates of his birth and death and his views on social, religious and political questions. But this curiosity is not satisfied by any internal or external evidence. To make matters worse, there lived not only one author by name of Kālidāsa, but at least three known to Rājashekhara, who wrote :—

एकोऽपि जीयते हन्त कालिदासो न केनचित् ।
शृंगारे ललितोद्गारे कालिदासत्रयी किमु ॥

Aufrecht (Oxford Cat. Kālidāsa) enumerated fourteen authors whose lives and works came to be confounded and ascribed to the name of the greatest poet of India. The consequence has been, therefore, confusion worse confounded. He is made a toy of fortune, some regarding him as a Brāhman orphan, while others placing him upon a royal throne. Barring one or two traditions, others are simply absurd; but they show the popularity the poet enjoyed even in the remotest part of India. He has been also tossed between the eighth century B.C. to the eleventh century A.D. Rarely have geniuses suffered a strange fate as 'the brightest star in the poetical firmament of India'. Some of the traditions to be given below are now so historically increditable that they deserve no serious attention; but they show a tendency of human mind to group geniuses together.

Various anecdotes, whose truth we cannot yet determine, are told in India. According to the most widely believed tradition, Kālidāsa was an ornament of the mythical King Vikrama's court in the city of Ujjain:

धन्वन्तरिक्षपणकामरसिंहशंकुवेतालभट्टघटखर्परकालिदासा: ।
ख्यातो वराहमिहिरो नृपते: सभायां रत्नानि वै वररुचिर्नव विक्रमस्य ॥

In the opinion of some, Kālidāsa was at the court of Bhōja Vikramāditya of Dhār who flourished in the ninth century and the well known couplet laments the decline of learing after his death:

अद्य धारा निराधारा निरालम्बा सरस्वती ।
पण्डिता खण्डिता: सर्वे भोजराजे दिवंगते ॥

According to the third tradition (Indian Antiquary 1878, 115) Kālidāsa was a Brahman by caste whose parents simultaneously bitten by a serpent left this world before he was six years old and his wife's name was Kamalā. He was then brought up by a cowherd till he attained to his eighteenth year. He had, therefore, no education but was brought up as a darling of nature. Bhīma Shukla, the king of Vārāṇasī had a daughter, Vāsantī, by name, who did not accept any body's hand unless he was well-versed in all arts and lores. The king also wanted to marry his daughter to a famous grammarian named Vararuci, but the princess considered herself too learned for this scholar. Vararuci, thus scorned, met the handsome cowherd by chance as he sat on a branch and began to saw it off. He brought this poor handsome and stupid boy to the Princess after impressing upon him that he must remain silent. So he stuttered only an odd word as he stood before the king, and Vararuci cleverly interpreted it as a wise saying. The youth gave no answer to question asked by the Princess, and Vararuci explained that he was above answering questions put by a girl. The youth was then married to the Princess, who soon discovered the deception. But the stupid youth paid tribute of flowers to the great goddess Kālī, until she rewarded him with a knowledge of grammar, logic and poetics (Ruben. 1954. 272)—the three braches of learning needed by a poet to help him write correctly, logically and poetically. The youth took the name of Kālidāsa, "slave of Kālī", as an expression of his gratitude. When he returned, home his wife asked him whether he had attained something –अस्ति कश्चिद्वाग्विशेष : The poet thanked her wife and taking the first words of his wife's question, he then composed the poems of the Kumārasambhava, the Meghadūta and the Raghuvaṁśa.

A fourth tradition says that Kālidāsa was an intimate friend of Kumāradāsa, the king of Ceylon. The king had a favourite woman. One day the king wrote the first line of a Śloka : कमलात्कमलोत्पत्तिः श्रूयते न तु दृश्यते. On the wall of her mansion and offered a handsome reward to one who would complete the second line. The poet Kālidāsa happening to lodge at the same house, completed the sequel : बाले तव मुखाम्भोजात्कथमिन्दीवरद्वयम्. The courtezan then, with a hope to get the reward, murdered Kālidāsa and demanded the prize from the King. Of course the King detected the deception, for he was familiar with Kālidāsa's art.

A later tradition among the Pandits, void of any historical truth, makes Kālidāsa a contemporary of Daṇḍin and Bhavabhūti (Chiplunkar's Kavipanchaka). It is said that Bhavabhūti composed the Uttararāmacharita and read it out to Kālidāsa. The later spoke highly of the drama but suggested the omission of one anusvāra from the point of view of poetic beauty.[1] Once Bhavabhūti made a harsh remark on women[2] to which Kālidāsa returned a splendid repartee.[3] Once the three poets were travelling together to visit the shrine of Shri Ranganātha near Shri Rangapuri in Southern India. Kālidāsa then recited a verse[4] in praise of the shrine; Bhavabhūti followed him and Daṇḍin brought up the rear.

A current story regarding Kālidāsa (QJMS, 1918, 277) is that once a poor and ignorant poet approached Kālidāsa and requested him to recommend him to the king to give him some money. Kālidāsa asked him to commit to memory some

---

1. Bhavabhūti had composed अविदितगतयामा रात्रिरेवं व्यरंसीत् ।
Kālidāsa proposed अविदितगतयामा रात्रिरेव व्यरंसीत् ।
2. मधु तिष्ठति वाचि योषितां हृदि हालाहलमेव केवलम् ।
3. अत एव निपीयतेऽधरो हृदयं मुष्टिभिरेव ताड्यते ।
4. ऐन्द्री पाटलयत्यलक्तकरुचामंघ्रित्विषामङ्कुरैराशां,
मौलिकिरीटरत्ननिकरैः पाशायुधीयामपि ।
पर्यङ्के पवमानतूलभरिते पारे कवेरात्मजं,
मुद्रा काचनमुक्तिदानकुशला निद्राति जागर्त्ति वा ॥

words of benediction.[1] The poor fellow went before the king and forgetting what he had committed to memory, uttered quite the reverse.[2] The king became highly incensed, but Kālidāsa saved the poor person by putting an auspicious construction over the man's words.[3]

Once a learned Pandit called Ḍamaruka challenged the Pandits to compose a verse the first words of which he puts before them :

अम्भोधिर्जलधिः पयोधिरुदधिर्वारांनिधिर्वारिधिः ।

Only Kālidāsa was successful in accepting the challenge and composed the following verse fulfilling the conditions:

अम्बा कुप्यति तात मूर्ध्नि विधृता गङ्गेयमुत्सृज्यताम् ।
विद्वन् षण्मुख सन्ततं मयि रता तस्या गतिः का वद ।
कोप्याटोपवशाद्विवृद्धवदनः प्रत्युत्तरं दत्तवान् ॥

(Indian Antiquary 1874:115)

The foregoing remarks unfortunately help us very little in ascertaining, his parentage, his personal life and other facts concerned with his writings. Is it true that Kālidāsa was poor and a cowherd ? Similar tales of simpletons who were taught by the gracious gods have come down to us. Do the elements of social critical thinking in his works originate in his early poverty ? These elements are in any case so carefully hidden that Indian commentators have not mentioned them, and presumably, therefore, did not notice them. One can thus not claim that the anecdote about Kālidāsa's early poverty rests on this social criticism. This would seem to indicate a certain genuineness, even though the details about the Princess and Vararuci are improbable for Vararuci is traditionally supposed to have lived much earlier than Kālidāsa. On the other hand, King Kumāradāsa of Ceylon is said to have ascended the throne in 515, and this seems to fit in with Kālidāsa's time, even though dates are often contradictory.

---

1. त्रिपीडापरिहारोऽस्तु ।
2. त्रिपीडास्तु ।
3. आसने विप्रपीडास्तु शिशुपीडा च भोजने ।
   शयने दारपीडा च त्रिपीडास्तु दिने दिने ॥

Presumably Kālidāsa was already well known in 473, for at that time a poet in Mandasor (which is near Kālidāsa's home) caused an inscription to be carved on the sun-temple, some of whose verses are modelled on Kālidāsa's (Winternitz, 3 : 44). If this were the case, Kālidāsa would have lived between Skandagupta's time (approximately 455-467) and Kumārdāsa's (515), but was already being imitated in 473.

Other indologists think that Kālidāsa had already lived under Samudragupta and (or) Chandragupta II (375-375, or 375-413), and that he praised the victories of these in his works and also that these two kings had taken the additional name Vikrama, at whose court Kālidāsa is traditionally supposed to have lived. These questions are still not settled and we must confine ourselves to the statement that Kālidāsa appears to have lived in the 4th century. Negative evidence also confirms this view, while Kālidāsa is imitated and quoted from Vatsabhatti (JRAS, 1984 : 186-7), there is no reference to his works or to him in any literary work or inscriptions before the 5th century A.D.

Ujjain is generally accepted as the place where he worked. Kālidāsa's graphic and accurate description, of the Mālavā country and especially that of Mahākāleshvara at Ujjayini and its surrounding places has led scholars to believe that the poet must have been a resident of Mālavā. His description in the Pūrvamegha of the coquettish women of Dashapura shows his greater acquaintance with the city of Dashapura than with that of Ujjayini. It appears, therefore, to be pretty certain that Dashapura in Western Mālavā was his native place.

Historically, Kālidāsa happens to be in the period of feudalism. It seems that from the 4th century onwards feudal ownership of land began to develop. But alongside this, marked elements of the old system (slave period) remained for a long time. Kālidāsa therefore pictures courts where there were many men and women slaves; in his "Mālavikā" especially this theme is predominant. His Kings are still despots such as would have ruled in India during the Slave age. How the new feudal relationships affected Kālidāsa's court circles, we still cannot say. We do not yet know which strata amongst the peoples of northern India were decisive in bringing in the new age. It can at any rate be assumed that the beginnings of the new social order in Kālidāsa's surroundings must have been marked enough to provide the impetus for his optimistic, forward looking attitude to life.

1.2. Kālidāsa's Works

The reader must be now naturally anxious to know what wonderful creations this great poet has given to the world. It may appear at first sight that the order of sequence is here reversed. The works ought to be mentioned first and then the life of the poet should be described. But it appears more interesting to create a suspense in the mind of the reader to know the 'master spirits embalmed for eternity'. As has been observed above, there lived many persons bearing the name Kālidāsa and their writings came to be palmed off upon the Great Poet. Twenty seven works of different kinds are ascribed to Kālidāsa. Out of these the first seven are unanimously accepted as the works of the poet.

The *Ṛtusaṁhāra* is most probably the first poetic child. It is in six cantos corresponding to the six seasons of year into which the year is divided according to the Indian calender. It consists of about 143 stanzas. It describes very graphically the natural beauty of every season and the sentiments aroused by it. It shows the author's minute acquaintance with the flora and fauna of Western Mālavā, and an appreciation of natural beauty, but suffers largely from repetitions. It lacks in artistic unity. Erotic passion runs riot in this poem and shows the immaturity of the poet's art.

The *Meghadūta* is a matchless lyric that the poet comprehends the secret of love and manifests complete fusion of music, imagination and feeling. There are about 112 strophes in the poem, the number varying slightly in various handwritten copies available. All the strophes are in the same metre called 'Mandā-krāntā'.

'Kumārasaṁbhava' deals with a legend of Shiva. Only the first part of this epic poem, which consists of eight cantos, has come down to us. The birth of the War God himself and his victory over the demons is not contained in this part, which only tells of the growing love of his parents, the god Shiva and the goddess Pārvatī. A latter poet composed a second part. Whether Kālidāsa himself left the poem unfinished or whether his second part was lost, is not yet clear. But even as a fragment this poem is worthy of high admiration.

The 'Raghuvaṅsha' similar in form but in content absolutely, different, is declared, by many Indians to be Kālidāsa's greatest work. The subject-matter is purāṇic-epic. It deals literally with the line, but primarily with the descendants of Raghu, an old mythical king of the city of Ayodhyā in the northern Ganges valley.

'Shakuntalā' is a drama of King Dushyanta's love for the hermit-girl Shakuntalā. Urvaśī's fate in love (Vikramōrvashīya) is similar to that of Shakuntalā. The poet deals ever and again with the theme of love and separation, again and again he brings about a happy reunion. In the drama of Mālavikāgnimitra, Kālidāsa sings of the love of a slave girl, for this she was during the time of drama, although originally a princess. Thus for this charming treatment of his favourite theme of love, Kālidāsa did not use a mythical, but rather a historical background, a court and events which took place about 500 years before his time.

Kālidāsa sang again and again of the pains of separation and the joys of love. But since he portrayed in his works the loves, despairs and happiness of truly different people, since he showed his lovers as lovable despite their faults, and made them genuinely, human and alive—for all these reasons he is to be accounted a great and warm-hearted poet who for more than a thousand years has inspired all those who have learned to know his works. And his inspiration will not fade either in his homeland India or anywhere else where the human heart feels the impart of true art.

1.3. Kālidāsa's Personality

From a study of the works we can form a picture of Kālidāsa's personality. He must have been born and brought up in a feudal atmosphere congenial to the study of both sacred lore and secular sciences like *politics*, *erotics*, and *ethics*. His superstitious society did much more for the arts. The views expressed by Kālidāsa show clearly his attitude to the way his art clashed with feudal rationalism and the prosaic everyday life of the feudal society.

Feudal India of Kālidāsa was a progressive country in comparison with most of the rest of World, dominated by political reaction. It was in this that Indian people produced not only the secular science like dramaturgy, erotics, medicine, and metrics, but also the philosophical catecisms and law codes. On the literary side, it was left to the genius of Kālidāsa to become a prophet of the new synthesis in the stimmering ideas of his age and to give a new status to Sanskrit language. If Sanskrit came to be recognised as a national language all over the country, it was in no small measure due to the grace and finish that Kālidāsa contributed to it. In his period Indian art and especially literature were in the very forefront of world culture.

It would obviously be a fruitless task to set up Kālidāsa "in order of greatness" or create a kind of ladder with different rungs for Kālidāsa according to the place he fills in the development of art. We could never prove, nor would we ever need to, who was "greater" : Kālidāsa or Shakespeare, although this does not make it impossible or unnecessary to value differently the role and significance of Kālidāsa. We could never compare the value of the work of Kālidāsa with that of Shakespeare, while we can see obvious differences between the work of Kālidāsa and Shakespeare from the point of view of artistry and from that of their historical significance. "Conflict for Shakespeare is the essence of the play, and harmony is always superficial and precarious. While for Kālidāsa it is the harmony within the rhythm of life that is the essence of play and conflict is but a peripheral skirmish." (Joseph, T.F. Jordens, "Idyll and Reality in the Shakuntalā and the Tempest." Jadavapur Journal of Comparative Literature, Vol. 5, 1965, pp. 1-21). The fact of such comparisons, however, does make the work of Kālidāsa or of Shakespeare lose any of its own aesthetic value, it still has the power to attract the reader. Or we could cite another, more complex example of the same thing. There could we do doubting that Kālidāsa's contribution to Indian and world literature is more significant than that of, say, Bhavabhūti. Inspite of his, however, Bhavabhūti's works are still rightly considered classics. On the other hand to compare Kālidāsa with Bhavabhūti could not lead to any serious conclusions on the superiority of either one or the other composer.

Comparison, however, is often not only possible, but even necessary, and this is a fact that will always be with us. It does not follow, though, that we should base our understanding of the concept of artistic progress on some idea of the superiority of the artists of one age or another over their precursors or their contemporaries, or adhere to these principles of "greater" and "lesser."

The idea that the works of Kālidāsa will keep their aesthetic value for many ages to come is itself a proof of the progressive currents in Kālidāsa. There is a continuous process in his works where previous forms do not disappear completely. They still continue to exist, alongside the other forms which have evolved out of them. In contrast to the world of nature, not only his works continue to exist and to excite profound interest, but also they cannot be viewed as lower forms in comparison with the works of subsequent ages. Movement from lower to higher cannot be regarded as the criterion of artistic development.

The development or progress that takes place in the works of Kālidāsa is the Indian tradition or continuity. The interaction of tradition and innovation (पुराणमित्येव न साधु सर्वम् etc.) has not only shaped the historical evolution of his art, but also has significantly contributed to his aesthetic achievements. Briefly, it is the general idea of "dharma" itself which is the undying core of Kālidāsa and Indian social tradition :— धर्मो रक्षति रक्षितः ।

Admitting the significance of tradition and continuity with the undying core of "dharma", we should accept that 'dharma' in art of Kālidāsa is not something detached from its forward movement, but along with tradition it appears as one of the elements of movement, because it heralds the appearance of something new. We should not confuse Indian tradition with stagnation, as Indian sociologists do. But if tradition goes hand in hand with the appearance of new forms and processes (न चापि काव्यं नवमित्यवद्यम्), and this is a fact in Kālidāsa which could hardly be but to doubt. then there is no justification to call that there is no progressive development in the art of Kālidāsa.

Of course, Indian art of one period is not isolated from that of others. To disregard the continuity between them, their harmony and the foreward movement means to ignore the facts which it is impossible to doubt. Great works of art from any period do not comprise a hermetic aesthetic world, whether in their origins or in their active life.

Kālidāsa's artistic progress may be seen as a process in which the study of life through images, grows broader and more complex and where new facets of reality are assimilated into the human imagination.

Artistic discoveries are to be made not only in spheres that are completely uncharted, but also in those fields that have already been more or less assimilated by artists. Kālidāsa is often quoted in this context, as a writer who while using the themes and plots of Epics and Purāṇas created new characters of unusual power, far greater in value than all those upon which they were based.

Another important feature of the works of Kālidāsa is that they are the best examples of comic traditions in folk culture and rose to the level of the greatest literature of the age, impregnating it with their strength. Without understanding this fact, we can understand neither the literature nor the culture of the Gupta age.

Significant in the works of Kālidāsa is the depiction of character with a gradual development from the earth to the heaven. He develops his character through the ordeals of duties and obligations and not through rights and privileges. He strikes harmony among different aims of life. He believes in the growth of integrated personality. The high value which Kālidāsa placed on the faculty of reason does not prevent him from depicting burning passions of Rāvaṇa (Raghuvaṅsha, X) and the stormy of development of action. In the best of his works female characters are successfully depicted.

Kālidāsa found his plots and heroes mainly in the world of classical history and mythology. There is no doubting, however, the vital link between his works and the time he lived in. In India Kālidāsa arose against the background of a worsening crisis for feudal society, in an age of absolutism determined to subjugate both art and literature to its influence, a time when ideas and social or political movements were developing. opposed to both feudalism and absolutism. The historical and artistic meaning of the best works of Kālidāsa lies in the lofty examples, he gave us of human behaviour, in his criticism of spiritual and moral collapse and his condemnation of all kinds of particularism from general principles in the life of men and his call to social activity—dharma.

Kālidāsa is a representative of ancient Indian culture and a great upholder of social moral values, in the light of which he leads man to perfection. He is a great lover of humanity and to him, man is the best creation of the creator and so men on earth are happier than gods in heaven. His works are not only made for people and to fulfil their spiritual and aesthetic needs, but they are created to a perfect man and society, so that what is human in man may prevail over what is base and cruel within us. The objective meaning of his greatest artistic achievements is the defence of man and his rights, the defence of social justice and the true flowering of the individual's creative powers.

This orientation determined his art to move forward along progressive lines. And whenever, for whatever reason, his art abandoned the study of great human and social problems it came to a period of crisis and degradation. The evolution of Kālidāsa's literature is determined not by those who would dehumanise it, nor by those who support the idea of empty experiments in form, but by Indologists who are closely linked with this Great Tradition and seek to contribute something active to the transformation of society and to the development of the ideal man of Kālidāsa.

1.4. Methodology of Analysis

The very emergence of literary semantics, as well as semantic philosophy as a whole, is largely due to the need of traditional ideology for the study of Kālidāsa capable of replacing the traditional school of subjective idealism, which has become defunct in this technological age, and proved incapable of answering the questions posed by new scientific cognition. Analysis was needed which would be able to serve beneath the banner of science without breaking with idealism—the dominant world-view of the then feudal society.

In this analysis of literary semantics we proceed from the principle that subjectivism is the dominant tendency in all contemporary Sanskrit scholars of India. This does not mean that objective idealism has lost its significance in modern India, but that it reveals an increasingly marked tendency towards subjectivism.

This characterization is fully borne out by an analysis of the trend in literary criticism in modern Indologists. This trend has acquired a different import with the entry of capitalism into the state of intellectual imperialism in India.

The main task of the present book is to discern in each system the determinations themselves, the actual crystallisation pervading the whole literary genre of Kālidāsa. One such motif in the literary semantics is the fact that language is also an object or literary study, to the premise that it is its only object of study. O the basis of this theoretical principle attention is being paid predominantly to the possibility of using procedures of linguistic analysis in the study of Kālidāsa. This has created the basis for the extensive use of logical and mathematical apparatus in different fields of literary criticism.

The second methodological task of the present study is to show how and to what purpose the literary semantics relates to scientific cognition. The present stage in the development of scientific research is characterized by the intensive adoption of the exact methods of research of natural sciences and mathematics by the humanities. The emergence of such new special scientific disciplines as semiotics, information theory etc. has stimulated scholars to apply these principles and methods in their literary studies. Exact methods of research enables us to attain important theoretical results. A number of attempts have been made here to apply semiotic and structural principles and methods in the analysis of Kālidāsa's art.

The literary semantics of Kālidāsa, which is based on the methodological principles of semantic idealism, is characterized by a view of art as language, not from some aspect or other, but as a whole, from the point of view of its essence. This literary interpretation of Kālidāsa's language leads to a situation where as a rule literary semantics practically functions as a semantic philosophy of art.

2

INFORMATION THEORY AND WORDCOUNT MATHEMATICS

2.1. The importance of statistical studies in any branch of science, humanities or Social Science, cannot be under-estimated. It is sometimes impossible to proceed further in study without atleast, a fair statistical picture of the data on which one is working. The need for statistical studies is all the more felt, particularly, in creative works, where one's abstract design is bound to mislead for want of proper numerical calculations. Kālidāsa's works are not an exception to it.

The statistical study of the Language of Kālidāsa can be conducted in two ways. We may analyse the sample of occurrences according to their grammatical and lexical parts; and thus obtain the overall contribution of the two components to the language structure. In doing this, the mutual arrangement of the two parts is, disturbed. Alternatively, we would like to preserve the linear arrangement while performing a counting experiment.

The description of Kālidāsian language requires that the two components, lexical and grammatical, are shown in their linear arrangement in regard to one another. This will lead to the concept of the surface of separation, or the interface, between the lexical and the grammatical part, as to characteristic property of the language. As a two dimensional concepts, it replaces, at this stage of enquiry, the concept of the dividing point or line which is implied in the determination of overall proportions obtained for the two components, total and classified according to word-occurrence.

The objects or occasions shown by a particular word are by no means identical; there will be variations, sometimes quite considerable ones, between these objects or occasions which the use of the word enables us to disregard or to neglect as irrelevant. This is the very essence of the use of concepts or word-engrams. The greater the range of such variations, the often will there be occasion for the use of particular word, and the frequency of occurrence can, therefore, serve as a measure of the importance which the denoted objects have for our word picture.

In order to have a scientific understanding of the language structure of Kālidāsa, the stylo-statistical analysis is done in the following lines. This picture has been framed on the basis of word-counting, i.e. by counting of the occurrences of particular word in all the texts of Kālidāsa. The statistical condensation of this material is effected by grouping words, according to the same number of occurrences in one class, which leads to the frequency distribution of words, used once, twice, three times and so on.

The following table gives an idea of word-occurrence required for expressing the wealth of thought in the works written by Kālidāsa.

TABLE 1

Sr. No.	Sanskrit-Text	No. of Sanskrit Words
1.	Ṛtusaṁhāra	1319
2.	Meghadūta	1776
3.	Kumārasaṁbhava	4102
4.	Raghuvaṅsha	11102
5.	Shakuntalā	4173
6.	Mālavikāgnimitra	2041
7.	Vikramōrvashīya	2330

Several parameters have been proposed for characterizing the stylistic analysis. Before giving some rather extensive studies of the relationships between different style variables, we shall make an inventory of variables implied in a sensible and convenient way for grouping the words in the present context.

Vocabulary Measures

There are three types of vocabulary measures that have caught the attention of quantitative stylistician : vocabulary variability, the use of exceptional words and key words.

Vocabulary variability relates to a particular author's size of active vocabulary or to his ability or willingness not to repeat words but rather seek synonyms. Of course, it might also be regarded as a measure of non-redundancy.

The class of exceptional words may include infrequent words, neologism, technical words, or words of other foreign origin used to handle situations, or to refer to significates, so infrequently as not to be covered by ready words. It will be of interest to mention here that we have combined the vocabulary of active words and exceptional words in the present graphic analysis.

The term key-words refers to the specific word that an author uses at an unusual frequency ; but we have also listed under the title key-words those words which are repeated more than once. As the active vocabulary of Kālidāsa is very extensive, we have confined ourselves to the listing of key words only. By presenting the stylo-statistical data on Kālidāsa, one of our objectives has been to attract the attention of the scholars of other disciplines to this field.

The following table summarizes the complete vocabulary of Kālidāsa.

TABLE 2

Languages	Total occurr-ences of words	Total No. of voca-bulary	Percentage of words on total occurr-ences	Percentage of words on total vocabulary
Sanskrit	27,175	21,569	74.28	84.25
Prakrit	9,360	4,035	25.72	15.75
Total	36,535	25,604	100	100

From the above table it is obvious that the ratio of Prakrit words in the total vocabulary of Kālidāsa is significantly less than that of Sanskrit words, which comprise nearly 85% of the total vocabulary.

The relevant data regarding Sanskrit words may be seen in the table given on page 16.

TABLE 3

Sanskrit Vocabulary

	Active and ready words (non-frequent)	Key words (frequent)	Total
No. of words	17,433	4,126	21,569
Total No. of occurrences	17,443	9,732	27,175
Percentage	100	42.75	78.3

The traditional grammar is still alive in modern stylistics. It has provided the frame-work for categorizing and counting words in the studies of stylistic structure. The following table presents the stylistic analysis in terms of part of speech of the key-words of Kālidāsa :

TABLE 4

Parts of Speech

Sr. No.	Parts of Speech	No. of words	Percentage
1.	Noun	1,924	46.50
2.	Adjective	657	16.20
3.	Verb	623	15.25
4.	Participle	558	13.25
5.	Indeclinable	185	4.50
6.	Pronoun	106	2.55
7.	Vocative	73	1.75
Total		4,126	100

The table shows a marked preference for the Noun so far as the parts of speech are concerned. The list of the key words categorized in the above table is given below in a hierarchical order :

List of the (Most Frequent) Key-Words of Kalidasa.

Frequency Category No.	Serial No.	Words (Pada)	Frequency of occurrence
1	1	इव	794
2	2	अपि	654
3	3	च	641
4	4	न	612
5	5	इति	543
6	6	स:	431
7	7	एव	410
8	8	तत्	300
9	9-10	ते, हि Two words of equal frequency	223
10	11	मे	182
11	12-13	किम्, तम् Two words of equal frequency	178
12	14	तत:	176
13	15	तस्य	170
14	16	सा	155
15	17	यत्	144
16	18	अथ	138
17	19	खलु	134
18	20	इदम्	121
19	21	तथा	120
20	22	कथम्	112
21	23	त्वम्	109
22	24-25	तव, माम् Two words of equal frequency	106
23	26-27	एवम्, तावत् Two words of equal frequency	102
24	28	तेन	101
25	29	पुन:	100

26	30	ताम्	96
27	31	अहम्	92
28	32	अस्मि	90
29	33	मया	89
30	34	अस्य	86
31	35	मम	85
32	36	इयम्	80
33	37-38	त्वया, यथा Two words of equal frequency	78
34	39	वा	75
35	40	विलोक्य	73
36	41	तस्याः	70
37	42	तु	69
38	43-45	तत्र, यः, सह Three words of equal frequency	66
39	46	अवलोक्य	65
40	47	प्रविशति	64
41	48	इतः	63
42	49-50	नाम, प्रविश्य two words of equal frequency	60
43	51	त्वाम्	59
44	52-54	किल, तस्मिन्, देवः three words of equal frequency	58
45	55	भवान्	57
46	56	अभूत्	56
47	57	अयम्	55
48	58-60	आत्मगतम्, इदानीम्, एतत् three words of equal frequency	54
49	61-62	एषः, सखे two words of equal frequency	53
50	63	अत्र	52
51	64	बभूव	51
52	65-67	मनः, मा, सर्वे three words of equal frequency	50
53	68-69	अस्याः, आसीत् Two words of equal frequency	48

54	70	राजा	47
55	71-73	असि, नु, यदि Three words of equal frequency	46
56	74-75	असौ, आत्मानम् Two words of equal frequency	45
57	76-80	अलम्, एनम्, कुतः, तौ, यावत् Five words of equal frequency	43
58	81-83	त्वयि, ननु, परिक्रम्य Three words of equal frequency	42
59	84	पश्य	41
60	85	अतः	40
61	86	सस्मितम्	39
62	87-89	अहो, पश्चात्, यत्र Three words of equal frequency	38
63	90-91	एनाम्, पितुः, वः Three words of of equal frequency	37
64	93-95	निष्क्रान्तः, प्रति, स्वगतम् Three words equal frequency	36
65	96-100	अस्मिन्, नेपथ्ये, प्रकाशम्, वपुः, स्यात् Five words of equal frequency	35
66	101-104	कः, कृत्वा, दृष्ट्वा, परम् Four words of equal frequency	34
67	105-107	आत्मनः उपेत्य,, स्वयम् Three words of equal frequency	33
68	108	किञ्चित्	32
69	109-114	अये, करोति, क्व, राजानम्, वयस्य, सहर्षम् Six words of equal frequency	31
70	115-122	अद्य, अनेन, इमाम्, निष्क्रान्ता, मयि,यस्य, वत्से, स्थितः Eight words of equal frequency	30
71	123-126	आज्ञापयति, नः, हृदयम्, अस्ति Four words of equal frequency	29
72	127-132	आह, उभौ, चकार, देवी, पुरः, वयम् Six words of equal frequency	28
73	133-137	अभवत्, आदाय, भवतु, भूयः, सद्यः Five words of equal frequency	27

74	138-142	जनः, पदम्, प्रथमम्, भर्तु, ययौ, Five words of equal frequency	26
75	143-145	भवति, येन, सम्प्रति Three words of equal frequency	25
76	146-149	अथवा, नूनम्, भव, सहसा Four words of equal frequency	24
77	150-152	यतः, रामः, सर्वम् Three words of equal frequency	23
78	153-156	चेत्, प्रिये, भगवन्, शकुन्तलाम् Four words of equal frequency	22
79	157-165	अर्हसि, उर्वशी, एषा, क्वचित्, अनान्तिकम् तथापि, धनुः, पूर्वम्, बभौ Nine words of equal frequency	21
80	166-173	Eight words of equal frequency आशु, चिरम्, तपः, देव, पथि, मुखम्, विचिन्त्य, साधु.	20
81	174-185	Twelve words having similar frequency अर्हति, अस्तु, एकः, गुहः, गृहीत्वा, तस्मै, फलम्, भवतः, या, श्रियम्, सुन्दरि, स्म.	19
82	186-195	Ten words of equal frequency उवाच, कर्णम्, कृतम्, गुरोः, दत्वा, प्रजानाम्, मालविका, यम्, शकुन्तला, हन्त.	18
83	196-218	Twenty three words of equal frequency अमी, अस्त्रम्, आयुष्मन्, आयुष्यमान्, इच्छामि, उच्चैः, केवलम्, गता, तैः, दृश्यते, नाटयति, पुरस्तात्, प्रजाः, प्रपेदे, भविष्यति, राघवः, विना, विहाय, श्रुत्वा, सताम्, समम्, सम्यक्, साक्षात्.	17
84	219-236	Eighteen words of equal frequency अपवार्य, अवेक्ष्य, उत्थाप्य, कथञ्चित्, काले, कुमारः, गतः, गत्वा, ददर्श, देव्या, निष्क्रान्ताः, मुनिः, रघुः, रथम्, राजन्, वचः, श्रूयताम्, स्वम्.	16
85	237-257	Twenty one words of equal frequency अयि, इत्थम्, उपगम्य, उभे, एत्य, कस्य, चक्षुः, तस्मात्, तपस्विनः, देवि, प्राक्, प्रियम्, प्रियाम्,	15

		भवेत्, मुहुः, यशः, राज्ञः, विदूषक, स्त्रियः, स्थिता, हस्तम्.	
86	258-274	Seventeen words. अन्यत्, इच्छति, कदाचित्, गतम्, चेतः, तिष्ठति, दिशः, नवम्, पत्युः, पयः, पिता, प्राप्य, प्रियायाः, भोः, वत्स, सपदि, सार्धम्.	14
87	275-300	Twenty six words. अकरोत्, अन्यथा, आर्ये, उपसृत्य, उभयोः, एकम्, कश्चित्, कान्तम्, कुरु, क्षणम्, तदा, ताः, तेषाम्, नृपः, पुत्रम्, पुरा, प्रतस्थे, बभूवुः, भद्रे, भुवः, मन्ये, वर्तते, विधिवत्, सविस्मयम्, स्थितम्, विहस्य.	13
88	301-332	Thirtytwo words अर्थम्, अवतीर्य, अस्माभिः, आहुः, ऋते, एते, करेण, गाम्, तस्थौ, तेजः, निनाय, निःश्वस्य, पतिः, पार्थिवः, भगवान्, भवता, भवन्तम्, मद्वचनात्, मध्ये, मनसः, मन्यते, मुनेः, रघोः, रूपयित्वा, विधिना, विवेश, वीक्ष्य, शब्दः, सत्यम्, ससम्भ्रमम्ः, स्थाने, हस्तम्.	12
89	333-361	Twentynine words अग्रतः, अङ्कम्, अन्तः, अवेहि, अस्मात्, आकर्ण्य, इमम्, इह, उपरि, कर्त्तुम्, का, कृती, गच्छ, गुणैः, जनस्य, जयति, दृष्टिम्, धिक्, पश्यामि, प्रणिपत्य, प्राप, प्रिया, प्रेक्ष्य, बाला, रामम्, शरीरम्, सर्वाः, स्थित्वा, स्वागतम्.	11
90	362-403	Fortytwo words. अपाम्, अमुम्, अम्भः, आश्रमम्, उत, उपपन्नम्, उर्वशीम्, ऊर्ध्वम्, एहि, कुमारम्, गते, गुरुणा, चक्रे, चन्द्रः, जगाम, जहार, तस्याम्, तान्, तिष्ठ, ददौ, दर्शनम्, दूरम्, दृष्टः, नार्यः, निशम्य, निष्क्रम्य, नृपतिः, परिक्रामति, पश्यति, पश्यन्, पादयोः, भगवति, भवती, भवन्ति, मधु, यदा, राज्ञा, लक्ष्यते, विजयताम्, सखी, स्त्रीणाम्, स्वाम्.	10
91	404-459	Fiftysix words. अनया, अन्तरम्, अवैमि, अस्माकम्, अस्मै, अस्याम्, आत्मनि, आददे, आसाम्, इन्दोः, ईश्वरः, उपस्थितः,	9

उभयम्, उर्वीम्, कुर्वन्ति, गच्छामि, चिराय, जयतु, जलम्, तदीयम्, तासाम्, ददाति, दिवम्, दिष्ट्या, दुःखम्, दृष्टा, द्रष्टुम्, द्वितीयम्, नक्तम्, नाट्येन, निशि, पृच्छामि, प्रभृति, प्रातः, बबन्ध, विभान्ति, भृशम्, मातले, मार्गम्, मुनयः, मेने, यथोक्तम्, योषिताम्, राज्ञाम्, रूपयति, वद, विदितम्, विदूषकम्, विषादम्, शरैः, श्रीः, सख्याः, सति, सन्, सुखम्, हरेः.

92 460-532 Seventythree words. 8

अङ्गनानाम्, अङ्गम्, अन्ते, अपश्यत्, अर्घ्यम्, अवहितः, आज्ञाम्, आत्मना, आदेशय, आननम्, ईप्सितम्, उत्थितः, उषसि, ऋषिः, कच्चित्, कञ्चुकी, करम्, कामः, कुलम्, केन, क्रियताम्, चित्रम्, जयसेने, जातः, तत्रभवती, तनुम्, तन्वी, तपोवनम्, ददृशे, दुष्यन्तः, नयनयोः, निष्क्रान्ते, परिक्रामन्ति, परिजनः, पुरम्, पुण्यम्, प्रतिभाति, प्रत्यग्रहीत्, प्रयाति, प्रयुक्तम्, प्रस्थिता, प्रायः, बहुशः, भरतः, भर्ता, भेजे, मत्वा, मनसा, मनसि, मरुतम्, मातुः, मुहूर्तम्, मूर्ध्नि, ययुः, याति, युगपत्, युवा, रजः, रतिः, राज्यम्, रूपम्, लक्ष्मीः, वने, वयः, वाचयति, व्योम, शृणु, श्रुतम्, श्रोतुम्, सती, सप्रणामम्, सुतः, स्वस्ति.

93 533-670 One hundred thirtyeight words. 7

अग्निः, अग्निम्, अङ्गना, अत्रभवती, अधः, अधिकृत्य, अधिगम्य, अनन्तरम् अनुगृहीतः, अनुष्ठितम्, अन्यः, अन्यत्र, अन्या, अभिवादये, अमुना, अर्थः, अवलम्ब्य, अवलोकयतः, अवलोकयामि, आः, आत्मा, आदत्ते, आभाति, आरोप्य, आश्रित्य, आसन्, आसाद्य, ईशः, उक्त्वा, उच्यते, उद्दिश्य, एतावत्, एषाम्, करोमि, कर्णे, कर्म, कल्याणि, कष्टम्, काकुत्स्थः, कुसुमम्, कृतवान्, गन्तुम्, गात्रम्, गुणाः, गौतम, चिरात्, चेतसि, जातम्, जातु, जीवितम्, तत्रभवतः, तदनु, तपसः, दिशम्, दृष्टम्, देवम्, द्वयम्, द्वयोः, धनुषि, धुरम्, निर्वर्ण्य, निवेश्य, निष्क्रान्तौ, पतति, पदवीम्, पपात, परितः,

परिव्राजिका, पातुम्, पुरस्कृत्य, पुरीम्, पुरुषम्, पुष्यति, प्रणम्य, प्रभुः, प्रमदा, प्रयान्ति, प्राञ्जलिः, बभाषे, बहुधा, वाष्पम्, भगवती, भयम्, भर्त्रा, भवितव्यम्, भुवम्, भुवि, भूः, भेतव्यम्, मघोनः, मणिः, मदनः, मदनस्य, महत्, माधव्य, मालविकाम्, मिथः, मूर्ध्ना, यस्मिन्, रथे, रत्नम्, रहः, रामस्य, लज्जाम्, लता, लोकः, लोचने, वचनम्, वधूः, वरः, वरम्, वशो, वाचम्, विभाति, विष्णोः, वृथा, शङ्के, शरणम्, शरम्, शशंस, शश्वत्, सखा, सखीम्, सख्या, सत्वरम्, सदृष्टिक्षेपम्, सनिःश्वासम्, सरस्वती, सरोषम्, सर्वः, सासूयम्, सीताम्, सुतराम्, सूत, सौम्य, स्मरामि, स्मृत्वा, हित्वा.

94 671-804 One hundred thirtyfour words. 6

अग्ने, अजः, अतितराम्, अद्रेः, अधुना, अमोघम्, अर्धोक्ते, आबभाषे, आयुषः, इरावती, ईश्वरेण, उत्तिष्ठति, उत्सृज्य, उपविशन्ति, उपविश्य, उपविष्टौ, उपस्थितम्, एका, कथमपि, कन्या, कामिनः, कारणम्, कार्यम्, कालः, किमपि, क्षणमात्रम्, क्षितिः, गङ्गा, गति, गतिम्, गुरुम्, चक्षुषा, चापम्, चारु, च्युतम्, छायया, जाने, तपस्विनाम्, तमः, तस्यै, ताभिः, ताभ्याम्, दम्पती, दृष्टिः, द्विषाम्, धर्मः, ध्रुवम्, नवः, नाम्ना, निगृह्य, निद्राम्, निवेदयामि, नृपतेः, नृपस्य, नृपाणाम्, पदानि, परस्परम्, परिक्रामतः, परिगृहय, परिवृत्य, पवनः, पादम्, पित्र्यम्, पुत्रः,प्रचक्रमे, प्रतिगृह्य, प्रतिनिवृत्य, प्रतीतः, प्रत्यपद्यत, प्रयोगम्, प्रसादम्, प्राप्ता, प्रियेषु, बलवत्, बहु, ब्रूहि, भवत्यः, भूपतेः, भूमेः, भोः, मणिम्, मदीयम्, मधुः, मधुरम्, मयूखैः, महीम्, मातलिः, मानसम्, मार्गे, मुखे, यतिष्ये, यथाक्रमम्, याम्, युक्तम्, रघूणाम्, रराज, राघवम्, लक्ष्मणः, लताम्, लेभे, वक्तुम्, वपुषा, वसतिम्, वहति, वाचा, विधिः, विभाव्य, विलासिनीनाम्, विससर्ज, विसृज्य, वृत्तम्, वेत्रवति, शम्भोः, शेषम्, संवृत्तः, सकृत्, सदृशम्, सन्तः, समक्षम्, सम्पदः, सर्वतः,

सर्वत्र, सर्वथा, सीता, सुताम्, सुराः, सूचयित्वा, सूतः, स्नेहात्, स्पर्शम्, हरन्ति, हस्ते, हृदये, हृदि.

95 805-1031 Two hundred twenty seven words. 5

अङ्के, अङ्गैः, अचिरात्, अजयत्, अंतःपुरम्, अतीत्य, अत्यन्तम्, अत्रभवतोः, अन्तरा, अन्यतः, अन्यम्, अन्वगात्, अपरा, अपहाय, अप्सरसः, अभिनन्द्य, अमंस्त, अमन्यत, अर्पितम्, अवस्थाम्, अवाप्य, असकृत्, आज्ञा, आदिश्य, आधाय, आयुः, आरुरोह, आरुह्य, आलोक्य, आश्रितः, आस, आस्ताम्, आस्ते, उच्चताम्, उदधेः, उद्यम्य, उपेयिवान्, उमा, ऊचुः, एकतः, एभिः, ऐच्छत्, कण्ठे, कण्वः, कथा, कथ्यताम्, कल्पते, कामस्य, कालम्, किमुत, कियत्, कुर्वन्, कुलपतेः, कुलस्य, कुसुमानि, कुसुमैः, कृतः, कृताः, गच्छति गृहे, गृह्णाति, गृह्यताम्, चकासे, चक्रुः, चरणम्, चरितम्, चित्तम्, चित्रलेखा, चेतसा, छाया, जगत्, जगतः, जगाद, जग्राह, जघान, जनम्, तत्क्षणम्, तदानीम्, तनयम्, तनयाम्, तपस्विभिः, तरुण्यः, तानि, तूष्णीम्, तेजसा, तेभ्यः, तेषु, ददृशुः, दर्शनेन, दर्शयति, दहति, दिवः, दूरात्, देवस्य, देवाय, देवीम्, द्विधा, द्वे, धनुर्भृतः, धर्मम्, धाम, धारिणी, धेनुः, नवैः, नारदः, निमित्तम्, निशासु, नौ, पत्त्रिणा, पथा, पदान्तरे, पपौ, परवान्, परस्परेण, परिष्वज्य, परेषाम्, पावनम्, पितॄणाम्, पित्रा, पुंसाम्, पृथक्, प्रजासु, प्रथमः, प्रभवति, प्रमृज्य, प्रविष्टा, प्रवेशय, प्रसभम्, प्रसाद, प्रायेण, प्रियया, प्रियाः, प्रीतः, प्रीतिम्, बत, बध्नाति, बलात्, बाणैः, भयात्, भवते, भवन्तः, भाति, भावस्, भीरु, भूतानाम्, भूमिः, भूयिष्ठम्, भो भोः, मनांसि, मनोहरम्, मन्दम्, मरुतः, महतः, महति, महर्षेः, महिमा, मार्गः, मिथ्या, मूर्खेन, मुखैः, मृगैः, मृग्यते, मृदु, मेघः, मोहात्, मौद्गल्य, ययाचे, यास्यति, यैः, योगम्, योषितः, यौवनम्, रथः, रविः, रवेः, रात्रिः, रूपयन्ति, लक्ष्म्या, लातव्य, वनम्, वयसि, वल्कलम्,

ववन्दे, वसु, वह्निः, वासः, विज्ञापयति, विदितः, विदुः, विमानम्, विलोचनानि, वीर्यम्, वृतितम्, वेत्सि, व्रजति, व्रतम्, शतशः, शशाङ्क, शशास, शशिनः, शिरसि, शोभाम्, संलक्ष्यते, संवृत्तम्, सखीभ्याम्, सदा, सम्भाव्य, सरः, सविषादम्, सानुजः, सायम्, सावेगम्, सुरद्विषाम्, सुषुवे, सेना, सृष्टिः, सोढुम्, स्तनेषु, स्तोकम्, स्मितम्, स्वः, स्वसुः, स्वेषु, हरति, हरिः, हिमांशोः, हृतम्.

96 1032-1404 Three hundred seventy three words. 4

अग्रयायी, अङ्गुरीयकम्, अङ्गे, अजस्य, अञ्जलिम्, अतिक्रम्य, अतिष्ठत, अत्रभवतीम्, अत्रभवान्, अधरम्, अधिकम्, अध्युवास, असङ्गः, अनयोः, अनु, अन्तिकम्, अपनीय, अपरः, अपातयत्, अपोहितुम्, अप्सरसाम्, अभिधीयताम्, अमात्यः, अम्ब, अयोध्याम्, अर्णवः, अलक्ष्यत, अवतार्य, अवलोकयति, अवश्यम्, अवसरः, अवाप, अवितथम्, अवेक्षते, अशून्यम्, अशेषम्, असंशयम्, असूत, अस्मान्, आकाशम्, आकाशे, आदिष्टः, आद्यम्, आपः, आयुधम्, आरम्भः, आर्तवम्, आवर्जितम्, आवर्ज्य, आवाम्, आश्रमपदम्, आश्लिष्य, आसनम्, आस्पदम्, इमौ, इयत्ताया, इष्टे, उत्थातुम्, उत्सुकः, उदन्वान्, उन्मुखः, उपगतः, उपगता, उपविष्टः, उपवेशयति, उपस्थिता, ऋद्धम्, ऋषीन्, एताः, एतावता, एति, कण्वस्य, कतिचित्, कथय, कथयति, कथयिष्यामि, कन्याम्, करः, करभोरु, कर्तव्यम्, कवेः, काचित्, कान्तिम्, काम्, कामिनाम्, कामिनी, कुतूहलम्, कुमारी, कुले, कुशः, कृशानोः, केवलाम्, कोपः, कौमुदी, क्रमात्, क्रिया, क्षणात्, क्षण, क्षणेन, खम्, खेदम्, गगनम्, गङ्गाम्, गजः, गणदासः, गणदासम्, गर्भः, गुणानाम्, गुरवे, गूढम्, गौरी, चक्रवर्तिनम्, चन्द्रम्, चरणयोः, चरणौ, चेटी, चेष्टितम्, छायाम्, जलद, जलानि, जायाम्, ज्वलति, ततान, तत्रभवत्याः, तत्रभवान्, तथाविधम्, तथाहि, तदनन्तरम्, तदा भृति,

तदीयाम्, तनुत्यजाम्, तपोभिः, तप्तम्, तर्हि, तात, तिर्यक्, तुङ्गम्, तेजसः, दक्षिणम्, दक्षिणेन, ददति, दधाति, दधानः, दर्शयन्, दातुम्, दाशरथिः, दासः, दिदेश, दिलीपः, दिवसः, दिवा, दिवौकसः, दिवौकसाम्, दिशि, दीर्घम्, दुरासदः, दुष्यन्तस्य, दुहितरम्, दृप्तः, देवाः, देवानाम्, देवेन, देहम्, द्याम्, द्वन्द्वम्, द्वये, द्विजः, द्विपेन्द्रः, द्वौ, धनुषः, धीरः, धुरि, धुरिः, नमः, नवेन, नागः, नामाक्षराणि, नित्यम्, निपुणिका, नियोगात्, निरूप्य, नीचैः, नृपाः, नेपथ्याभिमुखम्, पङ्कजम्, पत्नी, पदेपदे, परः, परिजनम्, परिणेतुः, परिवारः, परिव्राजिकाम्, प्रदोषे, प्रपन्ने, प्रसवः, प्रभाते, प्रभुत्वम्, प्रभाः, प्रमाणम्, प्रसूतिः, प्रापय, प्रवर्तते, प्रवासिनाम्, प्रविशतः, प्रविष्टः, प्रवृद्धः, प्रवेशकः, प्रसन्न, प्रसह्य, प्रियः, प्रियतमा, प्रीत्या, प्रेम, फलेन, बकुलावलिका, बभुः, बलम्, बाणः, बाणम्, बाहुः, बाहू, बिभिदे, बिभेद, बिभ्रतः, बीजम्, भवतीनाम्, भवत्यौ, भवन्तौ, भवामि, भानोः, भवः, भावी, भिन्नम्, भुवा, भूत्वा, भ्रातुः, मतः, मदीयैः, मनोरथः, मनोरथानाम्, मन्मथ, मरुद्भिः, महिमानम्, मही, महोदधेः, मातरम्, मारीचः, मारुतः, मुखानि, मेदिनी, मेदिनीम्, मेना, मैथिलः, यदपि, यद्यपि, यस्मात्, यस्याः, याचितः, यान्ति, यूयम्, रक्ष, रक्षसा, रक्षसाम्, रक्ष्यम्, रघुम्, रजोभिः, रतिम्, रथी, रम्भोरु, रहसि, राक्षसः, राजधानीम्, रात्रौ, रामाय, रिपून्, रेणुः, रेमे, रोचते, रोदिति, लक्ष्मीम्, लक्ष्यम्, लब्धम्, लेखम्, लोकस्य, वदन्ति, वधूनाम्, वधूम्, वनात्, वनिता, वन्यः, वर्तमानस्य, वसतिः, वसन्, वसुन्धरा, वाक्यम्, वाम्, वामम्, वायुः, वासवः, विदग्धे, विदित्वा, विद्धि, विधाता, विधाय, विधिम्, विभक्तम्, विभक्तः, विलोकयन्, विवादः, विश्वम्, विरुधाम्, वृषा, वृष्टिः, वृष्टिम्, वेद, वेलाम्, शक्यम्, शरासनम्, शरीरम्, शस्त्रम्, शान्तम्, शान्तिम्, शापात्, शासनम्, शासनात्,

शिरोभिः, शिरीरुहैः, शुशुभे, शृङ्गम्, शेषः, श्रियः, सखीनाम्, सखीभिः, सख्यौ, सङ्गतम्, सदयम्, सन्दधे, सपरिवारा, समये, समरे, सम्भावितः, सम्भाव्यते, सरसः, सरांसि, सरित्, सरितः, सर्वान्, सलिलम्, सवितर्कम्, सव्रीडम्, सशरम्, साधयामः, सायकम्, सारम्, साशङ्कम्, सार्द्धम्, सिन्धुः, सिषेवे, सुप्तम्, सुरगजः, सेनापतिः, सूर्यम्, स्थिताः, स्फुरति, स्मरः, स्मरस्य, स्रष्टुः, हत्वा, हन्तव्यः, हरः, हरस्य, हस्तौ.

97 1405-2131 Seven hundred twentyseven words. 3

अक्षिणोत्, अक्ष्णाम्, अक्ष्णोः, अगमत्, अगात्, अग्नौ, अग्रजेन, अग्रहीत्, अग्र्याम्, अङ्गानि, अङ्गुल्या, अङ्गेषु, अचलः, अजेन, अत्रभवत्याः, अदर्शयत्, अदृश्यत्, अद्भिः, अद्रिः, अधिज्यम्, अधिपतिः, अनुपपन्नम्, अध्वनि, अनङ्ग, अनुग्रह, अनुज्ञातम्, अनुत्ज्ञाम्, अन्तम्, अन्तरात्मा, अन्तर्गतम्, अन्त्यम्, अन्यस्मिन्, अन्वगच्छत्, अन्वभूत, अपटीक्षेपेण, अपश्यताम्, अप्सु, अब्रवीत्, अभविष्यत्, अभिख्याम्, अभितः, अभितापितः, अभिनीय, अभिलाषम्, अभिहितः, अभिहिता, अभूताम्, अभ्यनन्दत्, अभ्रवृन्दम्, अमृतम्, अम्वु, अम्भसाम्, अम्भसि, अरीणाम्, अरुन्धती, अर्थिनः, अर्थे, अर्पयति, अर्हन्ति, अलकैः, अवकाशम्, अवतरतः, अवतीर्णः, अवदद्, अवधूय, अवलम्बते, अवोचत्, अशोकः, अशोकम्, अश्रु, अश्रुभिः, अष्टाभिः, अस्यै, आकाशयानेन, आक्षिप्य, आखण्डलस्य, आघ्राय, आचकाङ्क्ष, आचख्युः, आजौ, आज्ञया, आज्ञापयतु, आज्ञापयन्ति, आतपम्, आत्थ, आदधानः, आदिदेश, आदेशम्, आनय, आनर्च, आपुः, आप्नुहि, आभरणम्, आभरणानि, आमनन्ति, आमंत्र्य, आयुष्मन्तम्, आरात्, आरुढम्, आलोक्यते, आवयोः, आविरभूत्, आविष्कृतम्, आवेद्य, आशिषः, आशिषम्, आश्रमवासिनः, आश्रमे, आश्वास्य, आससाद, आस्थाय, आहितम्, आहूयताम्, इच्छन्, इच्छसि, इतस्ततः, इन्दुः,

इन्द्रः, इरावतीम्, इषुभिः, इष्टम्, ईदृशम्, उक्तम्, उच्छ्वसितम्, उत्तरकोसलानाम्, उत्तरम्, उत्तरेण, उत्तिष्ठ, उत्थाप्य, उत्पश्यामि, उत्सवः, उदयात्, उदये, उदाहरन्ति, उद्यतः, उद्वहन्ती, उन्नमय्य, उपतस्थे, उपदेशम्, उपनतम्, उपपद्यते, उपयेमे, उपलभ्य, उपवनानि, उपान्तेषु, उपैति, उभाभ्याम्, उरः, उरसि, उष्णम्, ऊचिवान्, ऋत्विजः, ऋषयः, ऋषिम्, ऋषीणाम्, ऋषेः, एकपदे, एकरथेन, एकवीरः, एकेन, एकैकम्, ऐन्द्रम्, कण्वेन, कतमः, कथ्यते, कम्, करिष्यामि, करिष्ये, कर्मण, कर्मसु, कलशम्, कल्पः, कल्पितम्, कविः, कस्यचित्, कांक्षितम्, कातरः, कातरम्, कान्तया, कान्ता, कामी, कार्या, कुमारस्य, कुमुद्वती, कुरबकम्, कुरुतः, कुरुते, किन्तु, कुर्यात्, कुर्याम्, कुलव्रतम्, कुलिशम्, कुशम्, कृतापराधान्, कृतार्थताम्, कृतिः, के, केनचित्, क्रमेण, क्रिया, क्षमस्व, क्षमा, क्षितेः, क्षितौ, क्षेत्रम्, खे, गगनात्, गच्छसि, गजान्, गणैः, गताः, गभस्तिभिः, गवाक्षाः, गात्राणि, गिरा, गिरिः, गुरुषु, गुरूणि, गृहीतः, गोत्रभिद्, गौतमी, घनैः, चकमे, चण्डि, चण्डी, चतुरः, चन्दनम्, चन्द्रपादैः, चन्द्रमाः, चरन्ति, चरितुम्, चातकैः, चान्द्रमसी, चिन्तयति, चिरस्य, चेरुः, चोदितः, छत्रम्, जग्मुः, जननी, जनयति, जनाः, जन्तुः, जयम्, ज्ञातम्, ततार, तत्रभवता, तथाविधः, तदीयैः, तनुभिः, तनोति, तन्वीम्, तपति, तपसा, तपसे, तपस्वी, तपात्यये, तपोधनानाम्, तरसा, तर्कः, तर्कयामि, तापसी, ताभ्यः, तिरोदधे, तिष्ठतु, तिसृभिः, तीर्णः, तुभ्यम्, तुलाम्, तुल्यः, तूर्णम्, तृप्तिम्, तोयम्, त्यज, त्रियामा, त्वदीयम्, दक्षिणः, दधुः, दधौ, दन्तिनः, दयालुः, दवाग्नि, दशाम्, दिक्षु, दिनान्ते, दिने-दिने, दिवसाः, दीपः, दुश्चरम्, दुहितुः, दुहित्रा, दूरे, देव्यै, देशम्, द्वारे, द्वितीया, द्विषताम्, धनुषा, धन्विनः, धरित्रीम्, धातुः, धातोः, धात्रा, धीवरम्, धूमः, धृते, ध्रियते, नखैः,

नद्यः, नभः, नभसा, नभस्वान्, नय, नरपतिः, नलिनीम्, नवे, नहि, नागैः, नान्द्यन्ते, निचखान, निदधे, निदेशे, निधाय, निन्ये, नियोगम्, निरीक्ष्य, निर्दयम्, निर्वर्त्य, निर्वर्तते, निर्वर्तयामास, निवेदितम्, निवेशयामास, निशितैः, निशीथे, निषीदति, निहितम्, नीतः, नीता, नीत्वा, नीवीम्,, नृत्यम् नृपेण, नेता, नेतुम्, न्यवर्तत, न्यवेदयत्, न्यस्तम्, पटुः, पतत्रिणः, पतन्ति, पत्रम्, पथः, पदैः, पन्थाः, पन्थानम्, पयसाम्, पयोधरैः, परमार्थतः, परमेष्ठिनः, पराम्, परिक्रामितकेन, परिग्रहात्, परिहरति, प्रदक्षिणीकृत्य, प्रदोषाः, प्रपन्नः, प्रपेदिरे, प्रबभूव, प्रभावात्, प्रभुता, प्रभो, प्रमदाजनानाम्, प्रसूतः, प्रसूतिम्, प्रस्तावना, प्रस्थानम्, प्रस्थिताः, प्रहर्तुः, प्रहर्तुम्, प्रववृते, प्रवृत्तः, प्रवृत्ता, प्रवृत्तिः, प्रवेशम्, प्रसादः, प्रसिद्धैः, प्रापत्, प्राप्तः, प्रियंवदा, प्रियंवदे, प्रिय, प्रियतमाम् प्रियदर्शनः, प्रीतिः, प्रेषितः, प्रोवाच, फलानि, बन्धनम्, बन्धनात्, बभार, बलवान्, बलाकाः, बलैः, बहिः, बालः, बालकम्, बाल्यात्, बाहुभिः, बिभ्रत्, बुबुध, ब्रवीमि, ब्रह्म, भरतवाक्यम्,भर्तृषु, भर्तारम्, भवतीभ्याम्, भवत्योः, भवद्भिः, भवितुम्, भानुः, भानुमतः, भार्गवम्, भावि, भित्त्वा, भुजम्, भुजे, भूत्, भूपतिः, भूयात्, भोक्तुम्, भोगिनः, भो भोः, भ्राता, मञ्जरी, मणिभिः, मणौ, मण्डनम्, मत्तः, मधुम्, मध्यगता, मध्यमम्, मनीषिणः, मनोभवस्य, मन्दमन्दम्, मन्यसे, मन्युः, महताम्, महर्षिः, महाराजः, महिम्ना, महीक्षिताम्, महेन्द्रस्य, महौजसः, मागधी, माता, माधवसेनः, मारिष, मासान्, मुक्तः, मुधा, मुनिभिः, मुनिम्, मुमोच, मुहूर्ते, मूर्ख, मूर्च्छति, मूर्त्तम्, मूर्ध्नः, मृगः, मृगाः, मृगाणाम्, मृगेषु, मृदुः, मैथिलीम्, मैथिलेयौ, यत्नः, यथाकामम्, यथाप्रदेशम्, यथावत्, यदृच्छया, यन्ता, यस्याम्, याः, युक्तरूपम्, युद्धम्, युधि, युवयोः, यूनाम्, योगात्, रजनी, रतेः, रत्नानि, रथवेगम्, रथस्य, रथारूढ़ः, रथेन, रशना, राज्ञी, राज्ञे, राज्ये, रामेण, रुणद्धि, रुदती, रुरोध,

रूपयन्ती, रूपस्य, रेजे, रैवतक, लक्ष्मणम्, लब्ध्वा, लभस्व, लभेत, लभ्यते, ललितम्, लोकपालानाम्, लोकम्, लोकान्, वंशः, वंशे, वक्षसि, वक्ष्यति, वचोभिः, वज्रम्, वदनम्, वनस्थलीः, वनानि, वनान्ते, वर, वर्धते, ववृजे, वव्रे, वशिनाम्, वसन्ती, वसाना, वसुधा, वसुधाम्, वस्तुषु, वहन्ती, वाग्भिः, वाजिनः, वायवः, वाष्पम्, वासांसि, विजयस्व, विज्ञाप्यताम्, विद्यते, विधातुः, विधेः, विन्ध्यम्, विप्रयोगः, विभक्ता, विभोः, विमुच्य, विरराज, विलङ्घ्य, विलासिनीभिः, विलोचनम्, विलोचने, विवस्वतः, विवेद, विषम्, विषयैः, विसृजति, विसृष्टः, विस्मयम्, विस्मयात्, विस्मितम्, विस्मृतम्, वीक्षते, वीक्षमाणाः, वृतः, वृत्तिः, वृद्धिम्, वेदिम्, वेश्मसु, व्यतीयुः, व्यथाम्, व्याजहार, व्यापारम्, व्याप्य, व्योम्नि, व्रज, व्रजन्ति, व्रजसि, शंसति, शकुन्तलया, शकुन्तलायाः, शक्यः, शमयितुम्, शयने, शरण्यम्, शरत्, शरव्यम्, शराः, शल्यम्, शशंसुः, शशिनम्, शशिना, शशिनि, शापः, शाङ्र्गरव, शाङ्र्गिणः, शासति, शासने, शिखिनाम्, शिखी, शिथिलम्, शिरः, शिरसा, शिरांसि, शिवः, शिशोः, शुचा, शुचि, शुचौ, शुद्धा, शुश्राव, शून्यम्, श्रृणोति, श्रृणोतु, श्रृण्वन्, श्यामः, श्रिया, श्रूयते, श्रेयांसि, श्रोतव्यम्, श्वसन्, संयति, संयमिनाम्, संशयम्, सकाशम्, सतः, सत्याम्, सद्मनि, सन्ततेः, सन्ति, सन्तु, सप्त, सबहुमानम्, समग्राम् समन्तात्, समर्थये, समादिदेश, समीपम्, समीपे, समुत्सुकाः, समेत्य, सम्पत्स्यते, सम्भावयति, सम्भावयामास, सम्भृतम्, सम्भ्रान्ताः, सरयूम्, सरस्वतीम्, सरिताम्, सर्वस्य, सर्वैः, सलिलैः, सविता, सवितुः, सविस्मयः, सशब्दम्, ससर्ज, सस्पृहम्, सहचरी, सहधर्मचारिणी, सागरम्, सादरम्, साधारणः, साधो, साध्वीम्, सानुमान्, साम्प्रतम्, सिंहः, सिन्धोः, सिषेविरे, सुखानि, सुतनु, सुतौ, सुदक्षिणा, सुदुःसहः, सुनन्दा, सुमेरोः, सुराणाम्, सुहृदः, सूनुः, सूर्ये, सेनान्यम्, सैनिकाः, सौभाग्यम्, सौमित्रिणा, सौहार्दम्,

स्खलितम्, स्तनद्वयम्, स्तनमण्डलानि, स्तनैः,
स्थली, स्थितस्य, स्थिताम्, स्थिरः, स्थिरधीः, स्मर,
स्रोतसि, स्रोतोवहाम्, स्वनियोगम्, स्वरेण, स्वर्गः,
स्वेन, स्वैरम्, हंसाः, हंसैः, हन्तै, हर, हरिणा,
हरिम्, हर्तुम्, हर्म्येषु, हविः, हविर्भुजाम्, हव्यम्,
हसितम्, हस्तान्, हारैः, हिमालयः, हैमम्, ह्रिया,

98 2132-4126 One thousand nine hundred ninetyfive words of equal frequency 2

अंशवः, अंशुकानि, अंशुभिः, अंशैः, अंसः, अंसेन,
अकल्पत, अकस्मात्, अकारणम्, अगच्छत्, अगतिः,
अगारम्, अग्निषु, अग्रजन्मा, अग्रपादम्,
अग्रे, अङ्कितम्, अङ्कुशम्, अङ्गदम्,
अङ्गनाभिः, अङ्गरागम्, अङ्गवान्, अङ्गुलीषु,
अङ्गुष्ठमूलार्पितसूत्रशेषा, अङ्गेन, अचलम्, अजनि,
अजम्, अजस्रम्, अञ्जनेन, अञ्जसा, अतिथिम्,
अतिविस्तरेण, अत्यगात्, अत्यजत्, अत्यर्थम्,
अत्रभवतः, अत्रिः, अत्रेः, अथो, अदः, अदत्वा, अदूरे,
अदृष्ट्वा, अद्धा, अद्भुतम्, अद्यप्रभृति, अद्रिराजः,
अद्रिषु, अधरोष्ठे, अधस्तात्, अधिकतरम्, अधिकारः,
अधित्यकायाम्, अध्यासितुम्, अध्यास्त, अध्वानम्,
अनघम्, अनघा, अनतिक्रमणीयम्, अनन्यदृष्टिः,
अनपत्यता, अनयत्, अनातुरः, अनादृत्य, अनास्था,
अनिन्दितात्मा, अनिलः, अनिलेन, अनिशम्,
अनुगृह्यताम्, अनुजीवितः, अनुद्रुतः, अनुपदम्,
अनुबन्धि, अनुभूय, अनुमतः, अनुमन्यसे, अनुमीयते,
अनुमेने, अनुययुः, अनुरक्तम्, अनुरागम्, अनुरूपम्,
अनुवाच्य, अनुष्ठितः, अनुष्ठिता, अनुष्ठेयम्,
अनुसरन्, अनुस्मृत्य, अनेकम्, अनेकशः, अन्तःकरणैः,
अन्तकः, अन्तरायः, अन्तरिक्षात्, अन्तरे, अन्तर्गतम्,
अन्धकारम्, अन्यस्य, अन्याः, अन्यान्, अन्याम्,
अन्ये, अन्येद्युः, अन्यैः, अन्योन्यलोलानि,
अन्योन्यसंसक्तम्, अन्वक्, अन्वभुङ्क्त, अन्वभूताम्,
अन्वमीयत, अन्वयम्, अन्वयुः, अन्वयुङ्क्त, अन्वये,
अन्वास्य, अन्वितः, अन्वियेष, अन्विष्यति, अपः,
अपदिश्य, अपरम्, अपराद्धः, अपराद्धम्, अपराम्,

अपावर्तत, अपास्य, अपुष्यत्, अपूर्वः, अपेक्षते,
अबलाः, अभवन्, अभाषत, अभिजग्मुः, अभितप्तम्,
अभिनन्दामि, अभिनन्दितः, अभिनन्द्यते, अभिनवा,
अभिप्रेतसिद्धिः, अभिभूय, अभिमतः, अभिमतम्,
अभिमुखम्, अभिरुन्धन्ति, अभिलाषः, अभिवर्तते,
अभिषिच्य, अभिषेकाय, अभिराम्धाय, अभिसारिकाः,
अभिहितम्, अभीः, अभीषवः, अभ्यगच्छत्,
अभ्यगात्, अभ्यर्च्य, अभ्यर्थये, अमदयत, अमन्यन्त,
अमर्षणः, अमात्यपिशुनम, अमात्यम्, अमात्यैः,
अमूनाम्, अम्बरे, अम्बाभिः, अम्बुभिः, अम्बुराशिः,
अम्बुवाहम्, अयः, अयाचत, अयोजयिष्यत्,
अयोनिजाम्, अरमत, अर्कात्, अर्चिः, अर्चिषाम्,
अर्थपतिम्, अर्थवान्, अर्थिता, अर्थित्वम्, अर्थिषु,
अर्थी, अर्थ्यीभिः, अर्धमार्गे, अर्धासनम्, अर्भकः,
अर्हतः, अलकम्, अलकान्, अलकाम्, अलके,
अलकेषु, अलक्तकाङ्काम्, अलङ्क्रियते, अलञ्चकार,
अवगच्छ, अवगतः, अवगमयितव्या, अवगम्यते,
अवततार, अवतरतु, अवतस्थे, अवति, अवतीर्णा,
अवतीर्णौ, अवधीरणाम्, अवध्यः, अवनिम्,
अवरोधरक्षैः, अवर्णम्, अवलम्बिष्ये, अवलम्बे,
अवलोकयन्, अवसानम्, अवसिते, अवस्थासदृशम्,
अवस्थिता, अवहिता, अवाकिरन्, अविकलम्,
अविघ्नम्, अविनयम्, अविशत्, अव्यभिचारि,
अशक्नुवत्यः, अशनिः, अशोभत, अश्नुते, अश्रूणि,
अश्वम्, अश्वान्, अष्टमूर्तिः, असति, असमाप्य,
असाम्प्रतम्, असूयया, अस्तमिता, अस्मद्, अस्त्रैः,
अहः, अहनि, अहानि, अह्नाय, आकम्पयन्,
आकारम्, आख्यया, आख्यातम्, आख्याय, आगतः,
आगतम्, आगत्य, आगमनप्रयोजनम्, आगमैः,
आगवाक्षात्, आचख्यौ, आचचक्षे, आचरेः, आचष्ट,
आचारधूमग्रहणात्, आजगाम, आज्ञापय, आततज्यम्,
आतपत्रम्, आतपे, आत्तरति, आत्तशस्त्रः, आत्मजः,
आत्मजस्य, आत्मभुवः, आत्मभूः, आत्मसम्भवम्,
आत्मीयम्, आददानः, आददानाम्, आदधाति,
आदधाना, आदधानाम्, आदातुम, आदिशति,

आदेशात्, आदौ, आद्यस्य, आद्या, आद्ये,
आधत्त, आनृण्यम्, आपगाः, आपद्यते, आपन्नसत्त्वा,
आप्तवचनात्, आप्तवाचः, आप्तैः, आभरणैः, आम्,
आयतम्, आययौ, आयसम्, आयातम्, आयाति,
आरभते, आरम्भम्, आराध्य, आरोहति, आर्तस्य,
आर्द्राक्षतारोपणम्, आर्या, आलक्ष्यते, आलि,
आलिङ्ग्य, आलोकमार्गम्, आलोके, आवहति,
आविशत्, आविष्कृतः, आवृत्य, आवेगेन, आवेदयति,
आशंसे, आशङ्कते, आशंशसे, आशाम्, आशीः,
आशुगः, आश्चर्यम्, आश्रमः, आश्रमरागः, आश्रमात्,
आश्रयन्ते, आसनपरिग्रहः, आसन्ने, आसवगन्धगर्भैः,
आसीनम्, आस्यताम्, आहर्तुम्, आहिताग्नेः, आहो,
इक्ष्वाकुवंशप्रभवः, इक्ष्वाकूणाम्, इच्छन्ति, इच्छाम्,
इच्छामः, इतरः, इतरे, इत्थम्भूतः, इन्दुम्, इन्दुमतीम्,
इन्दुमौलिः, इन्द्रनीलैः, इन्द्रस्य, इमे, इयाय, इयेष,
ईक्षितम्, ईदृशी, ईप्सितः, ईशम्, ईश्वरम्,
ईश्वराणाम्, ईषत्, उक्तवति, उक्तवन्तम्, उक्ते,
उग्रम्, उच्चचार, उच्चारितः, उच्चैस्तरम्,
उच्छ्रितम्, उडुपते, उत्कण्ठितः, उत्तमम्, उत्तरः,
उत्तिष्ठन्ति, उत्तीर्य, उत्थितम्, उत्थितायाः,
उत्पत्य, उत्पाट्य, उत्सङ्गे, उत्सवम्, उत्ससर्ज,
उत्सहते, उत्सहे, उत्सृज्यलीलागतिः, उदङ्मुखः,
उदन्वता, उदारवाचः, उदिते, उदितैः, उदीरयामास,
उदेति, उद्धर्तुम्, उद्यतम्, उद्ययुः,
उद्यानपालिका, उन्नतैः, उन्ममज्ज, उन्मील्य,
उपतस्थिरे, उपादिश्य, उपदिश्यते, उपदेशात्,
उपनीतः, उपनीतम्, उपन्यस्तम्, उपरिष्टात्,
उपरुरोध, उपलक्षणम्, उपलप्स्ये, उपलब्धा,
उपविशति, उपविष्टा, उपसर्पताम्, उपसर्पति,
उपसर्पन्, उपसर्पन्ति, उपस्थिताम्, उपस्थीयताम्,
उपागतः, उपाचरत्, उपात्तम्, उपाददे, उपान्तिकम,
उपायुङ्क्त, उपारूढः, उपालप्स्ये, उमाम्, उर्व्याम्,
उशन्ति, उषितम्, उष्णरश्मेः, उष्णैः, उरुकीर्ति, उस्रैः,
ऊनम्, ऊरीकृत्य, ऊर्ध्वमुखैः, ऋतवः, ऋतुः,
ऋत्विजाम्, एकधनुर्धरः, एकपङ्कजम्, एकातपत्रम्,

एकान्ते, एतम्, एतानि, एतान्, एतौ, एषु, ऐक्षत, ओषधयः, ओषधीप्रस्थम्, ओषधीनाम्, ककुद्मान्, कटकम्, कठिनम्, कण्वाय, कतमस्मिन्, कथयसि, कथयामि, कथयाम्बभूव, कथाः, कथाम्, कथितम्, कदम्बैः, कदा, कनकासनस्थौ, कपिलेन, कपोलसंस्पर्शिशिखः, कपोले, कमनीयम्, कमलिनीम्, कम्पम्, कम्पेन, कयाचित्, करणम्, करणीयम्, करणैः, करि, करिणाम्, करी, करेणुभिः, कर्णेषु, कर्मणः, कर्मणा, कर्मभिः, कर्षन्, कलभः, कलभाषिणि, कलम्, कलापचक्रेषु, कलापिनाम्, कल्याणी, कश्चन, कष्टः, कष्टतरम्, कस्मात्, कस्मिन्, कस्याश्चित्, काकुत्स्थम्, काङ्क्षति, काञ्चनम्, कात्स्न्येन, काननम्, कान्तः, कान्ताम्, कान्तिः, कान्त्या, कामिनीनाम्, कामेन, कारणात्, कालस्य, कालिदासस्य, काश्चित्, किंस्वित्, किञ्चन, किम्पुनः, किम्पुरुषाङ्गनानाम्, किसलयम्, कीदृशः, कीर्तिम्, कुतूहलात्, कुपिता, कुप्यसि, कुबेरात्, कुमुदः, कुमुदम्, कुमुद्वतीम्, कुम्भयोनेः, कुर्वता, कुर्वती, कुलराजधान्याः, कुलोचितम्, कुशलम्, कुशलवौ, कुशली, कुसुमशयनम्, कुसुमायुधस्य, कुसुमास्तरणे, कुसुमितासु, कूजद्भिः, कूजितम्, कूजितैः, कूलम्, कृच्छ्रम्, कृच्छ्रात्, कृतसन्धानम्, कृताञ्जलिः, कृताम्, कृतौ, कृत्यवित्, कृत्स्नस्य, कृपया, कृशानुः, कृशोदरि, केकाः, केतकीनाम्, केनापि, केवला, केशपाशः, केशपाशम्, केशान्, कैलासनाथम्, कैश्चित्, कोकिलानाम्, कोटिशः, कौत्सः, क्रथकैशिकानाम्, क्रन्दन्ति, क्रमशः, क्रियते, क्रीडाशैले, क्रूरे, क्लान्तम्, क्षणः, क्षतः, क्षपाः, क्षमम्, क्षामम्, क्षिणोति, क्षितिपः, क्षितीशः, क्षितीशम्, क्षितीश्वरः, क्षिप्रम्, क्षौमम्, खेदात्, गच्छतः, गच्छतसु, गच्छामः, गच्छेः, गजस्य, गजाः, गजानाम्, गजैः, गणयति, गणाः, गतस्य, गतानाम्, गतिभेदम्, गतौ, गन्धः, गन्धवत्, गमः, गमनाय, गमयित्वा, गमितः, गमिष्यति, गमिष्यामि, गम्यते, गर्जितैः, गलन्ती, गलितम्, गाः, गान्धर्वम्,

गान्धर्वेण, गोपयामास, गायति, गिरः, गिरम्, गिरिम्, गिरिशेन, गिरौ, गीतम्, गीयते, गुणः, गुणम्, गुणान्, गुरवः, गुरुभ्यः, गुरुव्यथम्, गुरूणाम्, गुरौ, गुर्वर्थम, गुवी, गृहाण, गृहाय, गृहीतम्, गृहीते, गेयम्, गेये, गोप्तरि, गोप्तारम्, गोप्तुः, गौरवम्, गौरीगुरोः, ग्रहणम्, गृहीतम्, ग्रहीतुम्, ग्लपयति, घनाः, घनानाम्, चकर्ष, चकाशे, चक्रन्द, चक्रवाकः, चक्षुषः, चक्षूंषि, चचार, चतस्रः, चतुरिके, चतुर्भिः, चन्दनेन, चन्द्रमसा, चमयः, चमूः, चमूनाम्, चरणेन, चरन्, चरितार्थम्, चरितार्था, चलम्, चातकः, चापलाय, चापेन, चामरैः, चारुणा, चारुता, चिच्छेद, चिताभस्मरजः, चित्ररथः, चित्रलेखाम्, चित्रे, चिन्त्यताम्, चिरेण, चूताङ्कुरम्, चूते, चेतना, चेतसः, चेतांसि, च्युतः, च्युता, च्युतैः, छन्दः, छेत्तुम्, जगताम् जघनेषु, जनता, जनयन्ति, जिनस्थानम्, जने, जन्म, जयन्तेन, जयश्रियम्, जयश्रीः, जयोदाहरणम्, जरसा, जरा, जलदाः, जलार्थिनः, जहासि, जहुः, जाता, जाते, जानीते, जानीहि, जायापती, जालान्तरप्रेषितदृष्टिः, जितम्, जिष्णुः, जिह्माय, जीवति, जीवन्, जीवलोकः, जीविता, जीवितेन, जुगोप, जैत्रम्, जैत्राभरणम्, ज्ञानम्, ज्ञानमयेन, ज्ञायते, ज्ञास्यसि, ज्या, ज्योतिषाम्, ज्योतींषि, ज्वलनम्, तटेषु, तत्रभवते, तत्रभवत्या, तत्त्वतः, तदङ्गम्, तदन्ते, तदाख्यया, तदाननम्, तदीया, तदीये, तद्वञ्चितवामनेत्रा, तद्विधानाम्, तनयः, तनया, तनुः, तनुताम्, तनूजाम्, तनूनि, तन्वंशुकम्, तपसि, तपस्यति, तपस्यन्तम्, तपस्विकन्यकाः, तपोनिधिः, तपोनिधिम्, तपोनिधेः, तपोवनस्य, तपोवनात्, तपोवने, तपोवनेषु, तपःसाधनम्, तमोभिः, तरवः, तरुः, तरूणाम्, तरोः, तले, तल्पम्, तस्तार, तस्थिवांसम्, तस्थुः, तांस्तान्, ताडयितुम्, ताडितः, तातः, तापः, तापसीभ्याम्, तावता, तिथौ, तिलकः, तिलकम्, तिष्ठन्, तिस्रः, तीरे, तीर्थम्, तीर्थे, तुमुलम्, तुरङ्गम्, तुरङ्गैः, तुलयितुम्, तुल्यम्, तुषारैः, तृषा,

तेजसाम्, तेजांसि, तोयभरावलम्बिनः, तोये, त्यजति, त्रयः, त्रयाणाम्, त्रितयम्, त्रिदिवे, त्रिभुवनगुरोः, त्रियामम्, त्रिषु, त्रोतसत्रम्, त्वचम्, त्वत्तः, त्वदर्थम्, त्वरताम्, त्वरय, त्वरयति, त्वरया, त्वरा, त्वरितम्, त्वाष्ट्रा, त्वा, दक्षिणस्याम्, दक्षिणा, दक्षिणे, दग्धम्, दण्डकाष्ठम्, दण्डेन, दत्तः, दत्तम्, दधत्, दधतः, दधानाः, दधाना, दयिता, दयिताम्, दर्पात्, दर्भान्, दर्शय, दर्शयितुम्, दर्शयिष्यामि, दश, दशरथः, दशसु, दशा, दाक्षिण्यम्, दारेषु, दाशरथी, दास्याम्, दिगन्तान्, दिनानि, दिवसस्य, दिवसेषु, दिवस्पतेः, दिवि, दिव्याः, दिव्या, दीक्षितम्, दीधितिमान्, दीयताम्, दीर्घयामा, दीर्घिकाः, दुःखानि, दुकूलवासाः, दुनोति, दुरितम्, दुर्जयः, दुर्निमिते, दुर्लभः, दुर्वाससः, दुष्यन्तेन, दूयते, दूरवर्ती, दूषणम्, दृश्यताम्, दृश्यन्ते, दृष्टिपातम्, दृष्टे, देवकार्यम्, देवता, देव्याः, देशे, देहबद्धम्, दैन्यम्, दैवम्, दैवस्य, दोर्भिः, दोर्भ्याम्, दोषः, दोहदम्, द्वयोः, द्रक्ष्यसि, द्रक्ष्यामः, द्रवरागम्, द्रुमः, द्रुमाः, द्रुमाणाम्, द्रुमैः, द्वन्द्वानि, द्वारम्, द्विजम्, द्वितीयाम्, द्वितीयेन, द्विपानाम्, द्विरेफः, धनदानुजः, धनुर्धरः, धनुर्भृताम्, धन्विनौ, धर्मारण्यम्, धातारम्, धीरताम्, धुन्वन, धूः, धेनुम्, ध्यात्वा, नदति, नदी, नदीम्, नदीमुखेन, ननन्द, ननन्दतुः, ननन्दुः, नन्दिनी, नन्दी, नम्रः, नयनविषयम्, नयनसलिलम्, नयनानि, नयने, नयनैः, नराणाम्, नलिन्याः, नवकर्णिकारम्, नवपल्लवसंस्तरे, नवयौवनानाम्, नवयौवनेन, नववधूः, नागरिकः, नागाः, नागेन, नाटकम्, नाटयन्ति, नाटयित्वा, नाट्यम्, नाथः, नाथम्, नाभिः, नाभिप्रविष्टाभरणप्रभेण, नामतः, नामधेयम्, नारायणम्, नारी, निकेतम्, निक्षिप्य, निग्रहात्, निजगाद, नितम्बम्, नितम्बिनीनाम्, निदाघकालः, निदेशम्, निद्रा, निधीयते, निनिन्द, निन्दाम्, निन्युः, निपतन्ती, निपतिता, निपत्य, निपुणिकाम्, निपेतुः, निबिडम्, निबोध, निम्नाभिमुखम्, नियन्तु,

नियुक्तः, नियुक्ताः, नियुक्ता, निरीक्षते, निर्गत्य, निर्भिद्य, निर्ममः, निर्मातुम्, निर्वंश्य, निर्वृतिम्, निवर्त्तयितुम्, निवर्त्तस्व, निर्वर्तितः, निर्वर्तिष्ये, निववृते, निवारयन्ती, निवृत्तः, निवेशयन्ति, निवेशयामि, निशाकरः, निश्चित्य, निश्वस्य, निषङ्गात्, निषण्णः, निषीद, निषेवते, निस्तीर्य, नीपम्, नीलकण्ठ, नुदति, नृपम्, नेतुः, नेत्रैः, नेत्रोत्सवः, नैशम्, न्यस्य, पङ्कजानाम्, पञ्चबाणः, पञ्चमम्, पञ्चाप्सरः, पतिंवरा, पतिगृहम्, पतिगृहे, पत्रोर्णम्, पदात्, पदातिम्, पदे, पदेषु, पद्मम्, पद्मा, पद्मिनीम्, पन्थानः, पपुः, पप्रच्छ, पयसि, पयोधराः, पयोमुचा, पयोमुचाम्, परतः, परन्तपः, परभृता, परमर्षयः, परवती, परस्परस्य, परस्मात्, पराङ्मुखी, परान्, परावर्तते, परिग्रहः, परिचारिका, परिचेतुम्, परिच्छिद्य, परिच्छेत्तुम्, परितापम्, परिभूय, परिरभ्य, परिवर्तते, परिषदः, परिष्वजन्ते, परिहासपूर्वम्, परीक्ष्य, परुषम्, परेण, परैः, प्रदक्षिणप्रक्रमणात्, प्रदक्षिणार्चिः, प्रपन्ना, प्रफुल्लम्, प्रबलस्य, प्रबुद्धः, प्रबोधयति, प्रभवन्ति, प्रभवम्, प्रभवसि, प्रभा, प्रभाम्, प्रभावतः, प्रभुणा, प्रमत्तः, प्रमदवनमार्गम्, प्रमदाम्, प्रयतः, प्रयताम्, प्रयत्नात्, प्रयाणे, प्रयुक्ता, प्रयुज्य, प्रवर्तसे, प्रवालम्, प्रविशन्ति, प्रविशामि, प्रविष्टम्, प्रविष्टाम्, प्रवृत्तिम्, प्रवृद्धौ, प्रष्टव्यम्, प्रसन्ना, प्रसरति, प्रसवः, प्रसादात्, प्रसाधनम्, प्रसाधिकालम्बितम्, प्रसीदति, प्रसूय, प्रस्थानभिन्नाम्, प्रस्थाने, प्रस्थापयामास, प्रस्थितः, प्रस्थितम्, प्रस्थिते, प्रहरन्, प्रहर्ता, प्रहस्य, प्रहृतम्, प्राणाः, प्राणिनाम्, प्राणैः, प्रादुरास, प्रान्तेषु, प्रापुः, प्राप्तम्, प्रायशः, प्रार्थना, प्रार्थयिता, प्रार्थितदुर्लभः, प्रावृषि, प्रियंवदाम्, प्रियसखम्, प्रियाप्रवृत्तिः, प्रियोदन्तम्, प्रीता, प्रेक्षिष्यन्ते, प्रेम्णा, प्रोत्कण्ठयन्ति, प्रोषितानाम्, फणी, फलस्य, फलाय, फलैः, बद्धम्, बद्धा, बद्धुम्, बन्दिभिः, बन्धुकृत्यम्, बन्धुप्रीत्या, बन्धुम्, बबाध, बभासे, बभूवतुः, बलभित्सखः, बलवदस्वस्थ-

शरीरा, बलाकिनी, बलानि, बले, बहवः, बहुगुणरमणीयः, बहुना, बहुमता, बहुमानः, बाढम्, बान्धवः, बालस्य, बालाम्, बाले, वाष्पः, बाह्वोः, बिभर्षि, बिभ्रति, बिभ्रती, बुद्धिः, बुद्धिम्, बुधैः, बुभुजे, बृहद्भिः, ब्रह्मणः, ब्रह्मणि, ब्रह्मिष्ठम्, ब्राह्मम्, ब्रूत, भक्तिः, भगवता, भगवत्या, भग्नम्, भजते, भजन्ते, भद्रम्, भरः, भरणात्, भरतम्, भरताग्रजः, भरतेन, भवत्, भवताम् भवने, भवान्या, भवावः, भवित्रीम्, भवसि, भवस्य, भवेयम्, भस्म्, भस्मसात्, भाव, भाविनम्, भाषितम्, भास्करः, भिन्नाः, भिन्नार्थम्, भिषजाम्, भुङ्क्ते, भुजङ्गाः, भुजान्तरम्, भुजेन, भुवनत्रयम्, भुवनस्य, भूतये, भूतलम्, भूभृताम्, भूयसा, भूर्जत्वचः, भूषयन्ति, भेजिरे, भेदम्, भैषीः, भेष्ट, भोक्तारम्, भोगेषु, भोज्याम्, भ्रमति, भ्रमरः, भ्रमरी, भ्रमरैः, भ्रष्टम्, भ्रातृजायाम्, भ्रुवोः, मघवतः, मघवा, मङ्गलम्, मति, मतिमताम्, मदनेन, मदपेक्षया, मदिरेक्षणे, मदीयाः, मद्विधानाम्, मधुकरः, मधुना, मधुमद्, मधुलिहाम्, मधुश्रीः, मधौ, मध्यः, मध्यमलोकपालः, मध्येन, मनस्विनी-नाम्, मनीषिभिः, मनोज्ञः, मनोज्ञम्, मनोगतम्, मन्त्रवत्, मन्त्रिणः, मन्त्रिभिः, मन्दः, मन्दाकिन्याः, मन्दारपुष्पैः,:, मन्मथ, मयूरम्, मयूराः, मरुत्वान्, महत्या, महाक्रतोः, महात्मनाम्, महान्, महाब्राह्मण, महाभुजः, महारथः, महितम्, महीक्षितः, महीधरः, महीपतीनाम्, महीपतेः, महेश्वरः, माङ्गल्यम्, मातृकम्, माधवेन, माधुर्यम्, मानम्, मानसीम्, मानिनि, माया, मार्गवशात्, मार्गस्य, मालतीभिः, माहेन्द्रम्, मिथिलाम्, मिथुनम्, मिश्रकेशी, मिश्रविष्कम्भकः, मुक्तम्, मुक्ता, मुखमारुतेन, मुञ्चति, मुदम्, मुदितः, मुद्राम्, मुनिकन्यकाः, मुनीन्, मुमुचे, मुमूर्च्छ, मुहुर्मुहुः, मुहूर्तकर्णोत्पलताम्, मुहूर्तात्, मूढः, मूर्च्छन्ति, मूलम्, मृगम्, मृगया, मृगयाम्, मृगयाविहारी, मृगीम्, मृणालवलयम्, मेघाः, मेनका, मेरोः, मेरौ, मैथिली, मोक्षः,

मोहम्, मोहेन, मौनम्, मौर्वी, मौलिभिः, मौलेः,
यक्षाः, यज्वभिः, यज्वा, यथादृष्टम्, यथानिर्दिष्टः,
यथाप्रधानम्, यथाविधि, यथासुखम्, यथास्थानम्,
यथोक्तव्यापारा, यदर्थम्, यमः, यवनी, यशसा,
यशसे, यशोभिः, याचते, यानम्, यायात्, यासाम्,
यास्यसि, यक्तः, युज्यते, युयुजे, युवतयः, युवानम्,
युष्मासु, यूनः, यूना, येषाम्, येषु, योगिनः, योग्यम्,
यौवने, रक्षणविधौ, रक्षति, रक्षांसि, रक्षिता,
रक्षितुः, रघवे, रघुणा, रघुपतिः, रघुप्रवीरः,
रघूद्वहः, रचितम्, रजःकणैः, रजसि, रजांसि,
रणः, रणशिरसि, रतिविगलितबन्धे, रथवेगेन,
रथाङ्गनामा, रथात्, रन्ध्रेषु, रमणीयः, रमते, रम्भे,
रम्यम्, रश्मिषु, रसात्, रसातलात्, रागम्, रागात्,
रागेण, राघवाय, राघवौ, राजनि, राजपथम्,
राजहंसैः, राज्ञि, राज्येन, रामा, राशिः, रिपुः,
रुचम्, रुजम्, रुद्धः, रूपविधानयत्नः, रेवाम्,
रोधसि, रोषात्, लक्षितः, लघुः, लघु, लङ्काम्,
लताः, लतामण्डपे, लतासु, लवणम्, लिङ्गैः, लेखा,
लोकपालाः, लोकानाम्, लोके, लोकेन, लोचनाभ्याम्,
लोचनैः, लोभात्, लोलः, वंश्याः, वक्तव्यम्, वक्त्रम्,
वक्ष्यामि, वगाह्य, वचनीयम्, वचसा, वचांसि,
वज्रिणः, वञ्चनाम्, वञ्चितः, वञ्चितम्,
वत्सलत्वात्, वदताम्, वदति, वदनेषु, वधात्,
वधाय, वधूमुखम्, वधूवरम्, वधूसमीपम्, वध्यः,
वनदेवताः, वनद्विपानाम्, वनस्थलीम्, वनस्पतिम्,
वनान्ताः, वनाय, वनिताम्, वनेषु, वन्दे, वन्येन,
वन्यैः, वपुषः, वयसा, वयसाम्, वरतन्तुशिष्यः,
वरतन्तुः, वरेण, वर्णाश्रमाणाम्, वर्णैः, वर्तसे, वर्त्म,
वर्त्मनि, वर्धितः, वल्कलेन, वशम्, वशिनः, वसन्तः,
वसन्तम्, वसन्ते, वसिष्ठस्य, वसुमतीम्, वस्तु,
वस्तुनि, वह्निम्, वाचस्पतिः, वाच्यः, वाच्यम्,
वाजिभिः, वातः, वातायनसन्निकर्षम्, वातैः, वादिनि,
वानरैः, वामः, वामलोचना, वामेतरः, वामोरु,
वायुम्, वारोः, वायौ, वारिणा, वार्तम्, वाल्मीकेः,
वाहतक, वाहाः, विकृता, विकृष्यताम्, विक्रमम्,
विघ्नैः, विचार्य, विचिन्वता, विचिन्वन्ति, विचेष्टितम्,

साधुः, साधोः, साध्यम्, साध्वी, सानुमतः, सान्द्रकुतूहलानाम्, सान्ध्यम्, साभिलाषम्, सारः, सारङ्गाक्ष्या, सारङ्गेण, सारथिना, सावरजः, सिक्तम्, सिद्धयः, सिद्धये, सिद्धाः, सिद्धिमन्तः, सिद्धयन्ति, सिद्धयै, सीतायाः, सीमान्तराणि, सुखाः, सुगन्धि, सुतनुः, सुतम्, सुतस्य, सुन्दरीणाम्, सुप्तः, सुप्ताम्, सुभगः, सुभगम्, सुभ्रु, सुरबन्दीनाम्, सुरभिः, सुरभि, सुरभेः, सुरान्, सुलभम्, सुलभा, सुहृज्जने, सुहृद्, सुहृदाम्, सूक्ष्मः, सूचितः, सूच्यते, सूनृतया, सूनोः, सूनौ, सूर्यः, सृजसि, सेनापतेः, सेवते, सेवाम्, सेवावसरम्, सेव्यः, सेव्यताम्, सेव्यते, सेहे, सैकतम्, सैन्यैः, सोच्छ्वासम्, सोत्सुकम्, सोपचारम्, सोमः, सौमित्रिः, स्तनांशुकम्, स्तनाभ्याम्, स्तनौ, स्त्री, स्त्रीषु, स्थलीम्, स्थाणुः, स्थाणुम्, स्थापय, स्थापयित्वा, स्थापितः, स्थापिता, स्थावरजङ्गमानाम्, स्थिते, स्थितौ, स्थीयताम्, स्नेहः, स्नेहस्य, स्नेहेन, स्पर्शः, स्पृशति, स्पृशन्, स्पृष्टः, स्पृहणीयशोभम्, स्फुटफेनराजिः, स्फुरता, स्फुरत्प्रभामण्डलम्, स्म, स्मरन्, स्मरम्, स्मरसि, स्मरिष्यति, स्मृतः, स्मृतिः, स्मेरमुखः, स्युः, स्रजम्, स्रस्तम्, स्रोतोवहा, स्वजनः, स्वदेहम्, स्वदेहात्, स्वप्ने, स्वप्नेषु, स्वर्गाभिष्यन्दवमनम्, स्वल्पम्, स्वसारम्, स्वान्, स्विन्नाङ्गुलिः, स्वे, स्वेषाम्, हंस, हंहो, हतः, हतस्य, हन्तुम्, हन्मि, हरम्, हरिचन्दनेन, हरिण्यः, हरिताम्, हरिभिः, हविषा, हसन्ती, हा, हाराः, हिंस्रैः, हिमम्, हिमवान्, हिमाद्रेः, हुतम्, हुताशनः, हुताशनस्य, हृतः, हृताम्, हृदय, हृदयनिहितैः, हृदयस्य, हेतुः, हैमवतम्, हृदः।

The list of the words is now grouped again on the basis of 'Item-Frequency-Count'.

GROUPING BASED ON FREQUENCY-COUNT.

Items	No. of words	Frequency count of each word	Items	No. of words	Frequency count of each word
1. Forty six items	1	794		1	90
	1	654		1	89
	1	641		1	86
	1	612		1	85
	1	543		1	80
	1	431		1	75
	1	410		1	73
	1	300		1	70
	1	182		1	69
	1	176		1	65
	1	170		1	64
	1	155		1	63
	1	144		1	59
	1	138		1	57
	1	134		1	56
	1	121		1	55
	1	120		1	52
	1	112		1	51
	1	109		1	47
	1	101		1	41
	1	100		1	40
	1	96		1	39
	1	92		1	32
2. Nine items	2	223		2	60
	2	178		2	53
	2	106		2	48
	2	102		2	45
	2	78			
3. Twelve items	3	66		3	38
	3	58		3	37
	3	54		3	36
	3	50		3	33
	3	46		3	25
	3	42		3	23

Items	No. of words	Frequency count of each word	Items	No. of words	Frequency count of each word
4. Four items	4	34		4	24
	4	29		4	22
5. Four items	5	43		5	27
	5	35		5	26
6. One item	6	31	7. One item	7	28
8. Two items	8	30		8	20
9. One item	9	21	10. One item	10	18
11. One item	12	19	12. One item	17	14
13. One item	18	16	14. One item	21	15
15. One item	23	17	16. One item	26	13
17. One item	27	13	18. One item	29	11
19. One item	32	12	20. One item	42	10
21. One item	56	9	22. One item	73	8
23. One item	134	6	24. One item	138	7
25. One item	227	5	26. One item	373	4
27. One item	727	3	28. One item	1995	2
Total		4126			9732

It may be concluded that this study does not only provide patterns for similar works, but data given here may be used directly for further work according to the ingenuity of the reader.

From the point of view of statistical standards alone, the above figures present a clear picture of the expanse of Kalidasian language and the richness of his vocabulary.

Accompanied with the expanding nature of forms is the expanding nature of the meaning they convey. Each single form gives out a definite meaning, distinct from that of the other forms. The total number of forms thus gives us the total number of subtle semantic shades.

The semantic shades that each form throws are primarily on the simple plane of what is called the 'primary meaning' or अभिधा.

An expert writer like Kālidāsa twists each word to give out secondary meaning or लक्षणा, or suggestive meaning or व्यंजना and we have so many other semantic shades also.

2.2. First five most frequent words

इव (f. 794), अपि (f. 654), च (f. 641), न (f. 612) and इति (f. 543) in Kalidasian works are among the first five most frequent words. These are the important key-words that Kālidāsa uses at an unusual frequency ranging from 794 to 543. These words are typical but most beloved words of Kālidāsa. Morphologically these words fall under the sub-group of particles. Thus Kālidāsa excels in his love for particles.

As is well known, the term, 'particle' has been applied in very different ways by various grammarians, and a satisfactory definition has, as far as the ancient Indo-European languages are concerned, not yet been given. In Sanskrit 'the indeclinable words are less distinctly divided into parts of speech' than other classes of words : there are often, no hard and fast lines drawn, to identify adverbs, particles, prepositions. The same part of speech may fulfil more than one function.

The meaning of the common particle इव seems to be quite simple. However, the problems connected with its etymology and semasiology are rather complicated. The particle approves this general statement on Kālidāsa that he is a master-mind in the use of the similie.

In regard to Sanskrit element इव it may, generally speaking, be said that many authors of grammar and dictionaries limited themselves to a mere arrangement of the main facts ; i.e. what they call the 'meanings' or uses of the word, without entering into a discussion of the interrelations between these meanings and in all probability overlooking the fact that a variety of the so-called different senses of a word in Kalidasian language is nothing else but a translational difficulty in disguise.

The particle अपि has many meanings in Kālidāsa. Some of these meanings may be listed here :

(1) "on the other hand" ; c. f. न चापि काव्यं नवमित्यवद्यम् (Mal. 1. 2) 'every old poem is not good because it is old ; nor (न चापि) is every new poem to be condemned because it is new'.

(2) 'only, but'; c.f. एकेनापि सन्धिना (Shak. 5.61) 'only with this one understanding that.'

(3) "some etc." c.f. काप्यभिख्या तयोरासीत् (Raghu 1.46) 'some beauty was in them'.

(4) 'expression of doubt' (अपि शंकायाम्),

(5) 'combined with नाम अपि occurs in sentences expressing 'a wish, hope, probability, supposition, etc. : अपि नाम शकुन्तला स्यात् (Shak. 1.19) 'Can she be'.

(6) 'used concessively' in many cases,

(7) 'used generally as an emphasizing particle, sometimes before and sometimes after the word it belongs to. The emphasized word may be a noun, a pronoun, an adjective, an adverb or a verb.'

(8) 'अपि is sometimes eqvivalent to च' e.g. तव न जाने हृदयम् मम पुनः कामो दिवाऽपि रात्रावपि (Shak. 3.14).

(9) The particle is rather often used in the beginning of a sentence introducing question : अपि शकुन्तलादर्शने कुतूहलम् (Shak. 2.16). 'Are you interested in seeing Shakuntala ?' अपि तपो वर्धते (ibid. 1.22)) 'Does austerity prosper ?' Here it can be recognised by a special intonation.

Some more shades in the meaning of अपि may be found in the following examples :

(क) शठ इति मयि तावदस्तु ते
परिचयवत्यवधीरणा प्रिये ।
चरणपतितया न चण्डि
तां विसृजसि मेखलाऽपि याचिता ।। (Mal 3)

(ख) मेघालोके भवति सुखिनोऽप्यन्यथावृत्तिचेतः
कण्ठाश्लेषप्रणयिनि जने किम्पुनर्दूरसंस्थे । (Megh)

(ग) अन्तः शुद्धस्त्वमसि भविता वर्णमात्रेण कृष्णः (Megh)

(घ) छायात्माऽपि प्रकृतिसुभगो लप्स्यते ते प्रवेशम् (Megh)

(ङ) प्रजानां विनयाधानाद्रक्षणाद् भरणादपि (Raghu 1.24)

(च) न क्षुद्रोऽपि प्रथमसुकृतापेक्षया संश्रयाय
प्राप्ते मित्रे भवति विमुखः किम्पुनर्यस्तथोच्चैः । (Megh)

(छ) अपि प्रसन्नं हरिणेषु ते मनः (Kum)

(ज) अपि स्वशक्त्या तपसि प्रवर्तसे (Kum)

(झ) अपि सुखं सख्याः (Mal 3)

(ञ) जाते । अपि लघुसन्तापानि तेऽङ्गानि (Shak 3)

(ट) न स्यादन्योऽप्यहमिव जनो यः पराधीनवृत्तिः (Megh)

(ठ) भूयश्चाह त्वमपि शयने कण्ठलग्ना पुरा मे
निद्रां गत्वा किमपि रुदती सत्वरं विप्रबुद्धा (Megh)

(ड) भूयोभूयः स्वयमपि कृतां मूर्च्छनां विस्मरन्ती (Megh)

च (641 times used) is an exact equivalent of our modern 'and', and it should be regarded as a conjunction in the traditional sense of the term. Here are some of the examples of च which show its polysemic nature :

(क) अयमेकपदे तथा वियोगः
प्रियया चोपनतः सुदुःसहो मे ।
नववारिधरोदयादहोभिर्——
भवितव्यं न निरातपत्वरम्यैः ॥ (Vik)

(ख) मन्दं मन्दं नुदति पवनश्चानुकूलो यथा त्वां
वामश्चायं नदति मधुरं चातकस्ते सगन्धः। (Megh)

(ग) तामायुष्मन् मम च वचनादात्मना चोपकर्त्तुम्
ब्रूयादेवं तव सहचरो रामगिर्याश्रमस्थः । (Megh)

(घ) तां चावश्यं दिवसगणनातत्परामेकपत्नी—
मव्यापन्नमविहतगतिर्द्रक्ष्यसि भ्रातृजायाम् । (Megh)

(ङ) विषादलुप्तप्रतिपत्तिविस्मितं कुमारसैन्यं सपदि स्थितं च तत् ।
वसिष्ठधेनुश्च यदृच्छया गता श्रुतप्रभावा ददृशेऽथ नन्दिनी ॥ Raghu 3.40

(च) अपराधिनि मयि दण्डं संहरसि किमुद्यतं कुटिलकेशि ।
वर्धयसि विलसितं त्वं दासजनायाद्य कुप्यसि च ॥ (Mal 3.22)

(छ) अनुचितनूपुरविरहं नार्हसि तपनीयपीठकालम्बि ।
चरणं रुजा परीत कलभाषिणि ! मां च पीडयितुम् ॥ (Mal 4.3)

The negative particle न has been used 612 times. It has about thirty shades of different meanings. The न न variation of the particle sometimes makes an affirmative sense.

इति is known as a particle which denotes the end of a context or sentence. Apart from its function as a pause, it has other senses also. इति in Kālidāsa has twenty one polysemic load. Some of the examples of इति are as follows :

(क) पुराणमित्येव न साधु सर्वम् (Mal 1.3)

(ख) उमेति मात्रा तपसो निषिद्धा (Kum 1.26)

(ग) शिरीषपुष्पाधिकसौकुमार्यौ
बाहू तदीयाविति मे वितर्कः (Kum 1.4)

(घ) दिलीप इति राजेन्दुरिन्दुक्षीरनिधाविव (Raghu 1.12)

Although it is not possible to trace the historical development of the use of these particles in detail the fundamental unity of its so called senses is in, and through a large variety of contextual uses, clearly perceptible.

2.3. Test of Randomness for the word-length in mora and sentence-length

Sanskrit is a complex system with phonological, morphological and syntactical structures. In it, phonemes are its atomic units, and syllables are its molecular units while alphabets are the symbolic units. One may say that the Sanskrit vocabulary or the words of the different lengths in syllables or letters is the inventory of the language. The study of the distribution of phonemes, that of the structure of words in syllables or in letters, and that of the structure of sentences in words (or in syllables) are known as phonology, morphology and syntax of the language respectively. Each language has its phonology and morphology while writer has his/her own syntax. Writers, in general, take their choiceable words of different structure from the inventory at first, then arrange them in sentences and finally combine all the sentences of different lengths in words to create their literature. Because there is neither a standard method for the arrangement of words of different length in sentences (or in the whole text) nor a method for the arrangement of a number of words in sentences (or in sentences of the whole text), the line of thought regarding the pattern (or the occurrences) of the word-length series has been started with the application of the statistical methods. It may be assumed (or a hypothesis may be considered) that in a text/in the literature of language, the occurrence of word-length series as well as that of sentence-length series is random one. Herden (1962 : 25) writes "My contention is that the linear-sequences of linguistic forms in written text for speech are random series with respect to certain quantitative characteristics and any sampling procedure by disconnected linguistic units or by continuous pieces of text, or by pages or by chapter etc., will give a random sample of such a quantitative characteristics provided only that the sampling method is in no way connected with the characteristics, that is, provided that it does not consist in a direct or indirect selection of categories of just the characteristic we are sampling for." Hence it is felt justified in persuing the problem with statistical analysis based on the relationship between the successive values and the test of randomness of the said series.

The study of the measure of relationship between successive values of word-length in syllables ordered in space was first initiated by me (Allahabad, 1980). My contribution was based on seven texts of Kālidāsa with presumably of complete counts. My findings showed that the auto-correlation coefficient of first order between lengths of consecutive words in syllables. My findings show that the auto-correlation ranges from 0.010 to 0.162 with mean 0.045. I also considered the higher order auto-correlation coefficients, r_2, r_3 and r_4 for three texts of Sanskrit dramas.

The above study of auto-correlation coefficients enables one to appreciate the randomness of the series of word-length in phonemic syllables of Sanskrit literature surveyed ; while to discard the notion of randomness as regards the occurrence of the sentence length in words of the said literature. On the whole, one should not reach any firm conclusion about the coefficients (r_1) etc.

The text-study does not show that there is sufficient ground to conclude that some or all the literary works covered here have significant pattern of occurrences of word-lengths either in the sample or within the sentence. In other words, the arrangement in use of words of different syllabic length in Kālidāsa is elastic in nature while that of sentences of different lengths in words is plastic in nature. This is perhaps because of the fact that sentence length in a more genre-characteristic of the author than a language characteristic of Sanskrit.

2.4. Distribution of length

In this paragraph the statistical distributional patterns of the different characteristics of Kālidāsa's language such as word-length in mora and sentence-length in words have been summarized. This study reveals that the distribution of word-length in phonemic-syllables of Sanskrit follows more or less the law of Pearsonian system of curves while the distribution of sentence-length in words of the same text-literature follows lognormal distribution. It further reveals for the fitting of word-length distribution of Sanskrit Pearsonian system of curves is more close than Poisson fit and lognormal fit which were advocated by Fucks (1955) and Williams (1970) for European and other non-Indian languages.

2.5. Information-theoretic study

Herden (1956 : 66) writes "this branch of statistical linguistics of linguistic knowledge, inaugurated by De Saussure and Countenary, and developed by the Russian Trubetskoy and Jakobson, under the name of phonology, that the important thing about language is not the way it sounds, but how it manages to convey information. A great step forward in the study of this property of language was the advent of the statistical theory of information through which statistical methods which so far had at the best been appreciated as only an auxiliary tool of linguistic research were seen to go to the very heart of the problems of structural linguistics."

Shannon (1948) pioneered the methodology of the information theory and used it to draw certain conclusions about written English. His theory is based on the theory of discrete communication on a noiseless channel and its application on language is based on the assumption that language is a system for the communication of thought by means of symbols or codes as word-morphemes, phonemes etc. Based on this concept Shannon defined the amount of information given by the occurrence of an event X with a probability as

$$1(x) = -\log P_x$$

This amount of information $1(x)_m$ is itself a random variable and we can speak of the entropy (i.e the average amount of information conveyed by the observation :

$$H_1 = \Sigma_x P_x (-\log P_x) = -\Sigma P_x \log P_x$$

By convention, the base of the logarithm occurring above is taken as 2, so that the amount of information conveyed by the occurrence of one of two equally likely outcomes well be unity. This is defined a one 'bit' of information.

The notion of 'information' here deals with the permutations of language units providing meaningful communication and not with (by) the ideas and the feelings conveyed through as is the case in literary sense.

Shannon repeatedly insisted that his theory allowed us to measure the quantity of information, that is, a function of the rarity of certain symbols, and not to measure information in the ordinary sense of word. But others have been less caution, and the notion has been extended in the attempt to measure linguistic meaning, and even the circulation of information in society as a function of freedom, democracy and the like.

In this regard, Herden (1966 : 266) explains entropy with these lines : "As a statistical term it is quantitative concept. As such it is a measure of the case with which guesses can be made of missing part of a message. It is based not only upon word-structure, but also upon frequency of such structures."

With the appearance of the classical paper of claude E. Shannon (1948) many eminent scholars of science and linguistics stepped into the arena and made number of contributions explaining the structural character of language and writer.

In this section an attempt has been made to estimate the entropy of Kālidāsa's language with respect to the syllabic structure (of words) and word structure (of sentences) in the Sanskrit language. An examination of the data (vide Appendix) reveals that the entropy per syllable of Sanskrit language (Meghadūta) is 2.05 bits. The conclusive data as a whole the entropy per syllable for Sanskrit language of Kālidāsa works out to be 2.05 bits.

Comparing the values by Herden (1966 : 288) of entropies per syllable for English (0.76-1.56), German (1.65) and Russian (2.07-2.11) with the entropy for Sanskrit (2.03-2.05), one may conclude that the structural linguistics of Sanskrit language with respect to the language-unit as syllable occupies the place near Russian language.

2.6. Word-Count Mathematics

The term 'word-count' means the determination of the number of occurrences of the particular word by actual count used in a running text. The mathematical consideration of such material is, generally, performed by grouping of words according to their frequencies and the different words grouped in the above manner (vid. 4.1) give the probability density of the distribution. A work in this field was carried out by me (1980) under the head "Vocabulary Measures" and put forward same mathematical relations and principles of least effort under linguistic phenomena based on word-count.

The objective of this section is mainly to illustrate the various aspects of word-count analysis. This study reveals that Kālidāsa is highly rich in vocabulary treasure. Moreover, the author in his writing used 79 percent words which occurred only once, 11 percent words twice, 4 percent words three times and the rest 6 percent words got repeated more than thrice. There is only one word really outstanding in frequency of occurrence and that is, the commonly frequent "*Iva*" occurs 794 times. The other adverbs "*api*", "*cha*", '*na*' and '*Iti*' occur 654, 641, 612 and 543 times respectively. These are taken as the constants describing the vocabulary characteristics of the author, Mahākavi Kālidāsa.

2.7. Conclusion

The findings reported in the previous sections reveal a major phenomenon in the history of Sanskrit language in the shape of its poetry and drama. The phenomenon of structure change in the history of literature is explained by the (i) trend in word-length, (ii) trend in the proportion of parts of speech groups, (iii) trend in the proportion of sentence-length, (iv) trend in the entropy per syllable present in the different genre. This type of trend places Kālidāsa in the Gupta-age, as is evident from such types of trends in the inscriptional literature.

3

PRAGMATICS

3.1. It is an ambitious attempt to advance a theory of the pragmatic interpretation of utterances, drawing together on speech acts, formal semantics, and discourse analysis of the works of Kālidāsa. The analyses are based on the data of Kālidāsa, the attention given the role of social context in utterance interpretation makes the Chapter worth the attention of sociolinguists.

This chapter consists of nine sections, as forms of address, abusive words, the art of naming, paralanguage, kinship, folk-etymology and semantic change. The theoretical of much of the work is that of text grammar and involves a modular or componential view of linguistic cognition in which a text grammar interacts with contexts in a principled way.

In a way it is the interrelationship between language and society of fundamentally different sort. There are two basic kinds of socio-linguistic relationships that we explore here. The first of these concerns the relationship between language and society in the use of specific linguistic structures to achieve specified pragmatic-ends. It has been called by Hymes "the ethnography of speaking" (sections 1-4). The other relationship between a closed set of lexical items in Sanskrit and the cultural categories of the ancient people using that language is to be referred as "ethnographic semantics" (sections 5-9).

The term "pragmatics" is here used to refer to the study of the utilization of formal linguistic device to achieve describable consequences of the literary semantics of Kālidāsa. It subsumes a wealth of phenomena such as the use of fictive kinship terminology, circumlocution and euphemism, tabu, naming and various orders of poetic device. It also incroaches upon the stylistic manipulation of registers of language for particular purposes.

virtually a level of linguistic structure can be involved in the pragmatic use of language.

3.2. Proto-Feudal Society

By what name we call the social formation in Kālidāsa ? It is quite clear that it could not be slavery : it was Sudra labour, not slave labour, that was utilised for production. Was it feudalism ? It is true that there were feudatories under the Guptas with different titles and ranks. But they did not enjoy absolute ownership of land, most of the cultivated land being owned by peasant proprietors. Was it capitalism, then ? It is an absurd proposition on the face of it : the means of production, distribution and exchange did not grow to such a degree as to engender capital ; nor was Sudra labour free to choose its own profession. We can call it *protofeudalism.* Its main characteristics were similar to those of feudalism ; they developed into feudalism in course of time.

Being a citizen of the protofeudalism, Kālidāsa was liberal in his views on social matters. But at the same time he was not carried away by radical views. He was a conservative-liberal and wanted to retain what is useful in old institutions and adopt what was good in innovations (Māla. 1.2.). Caste system during his period lost its old significance. He does not appear to have approved intercaste marriages (Dushyant's misgivings as to whether Shakuntalā was a Brāhman or Kshatriya girl in the Shākuntala), though for inter-caste-dining he had no objection (the Vidushaka, a Brāhmana used to take food in the kitchen of the King). He was in favour of the four castes discharging their duties, but he was not against a Shūdra adopting the life of an ascetic.[1] The brāhmanas no doubt occupied a predominant position, enjoying mostly the patronage of kings and the charity of the public. Many among them were engaged in study and teaching. The Kings constantly sought their help in carrying on the administration.

The Kshatriyas continued to be the ruling caste. Latitude was shown to Kshatriyas marrying women of other castes. The Vaisyas were essentially traders with high degree of organisation. The Sudras who formed the bulk of the populations were mainly tillers of the land. The maiden-slaves were appointed in the palace. The group, on the other hand, was free to follow any tradition of cultural values without seeking to interfere with other groups though

1. cf.तस्मै द्विजतरतपस्विसुतं स्खलद्भि: । Raghu. IX.76

extending material co-operation to them. If these principles were logically followed, Kālidāsa had a universal society which was stable and harmonious without being static and uniform. The disinterested by concentrated performance of duty ensured material progress, while the aspiration for the higher led to spiritual elevation. Such a society was stable without being past-oriented and progressive without being future-oriented.

The position of women is often considered as a test by which the civilisation of a country or age may be Judged. The test is extraordinarily difficult to apply, more particularly to the proto-feudal ages, because of the difficulty of determining what in any age constitutes the position of women. The position of Kālidāsa's women is one thing in theory,[1] another in legal position,[2] yet another in everyday life. In the Kālidāsa's time, as now, the various manifestations of women's position reacted on one another but did not exactly coincide, the true position of women was a blend of all the three.

The fact which governed her position was not her personality but her sex, and by her sex she was inferior to men. We know that the ethical and social attitude to marriage was not much relieved by the specifically the feudal concept of marriage. In this way both Shāstra and aristocracy combined to establish the doctrine of woman's subjection, a doctrine which was apt to be linked with the notion of her essential inferiority, nothing matters that Kālidāsa presents the concept of "Ardhanārīshwara."

The idea of court-love could, however, go further than this. Its characteristic manifestation was not a general reverence for womanhood of Mālavikā or Urvashi or Shakuntalā and so on, but a wholly original concept of love which was to inspire much of the finest literature of Kālidāsa.

Courtly love as understood in this society of Kālidāsa had certain clearly marked insignia. In the first place it was held to be impossible between husband and wife. 'Marriage is no excuse for not loving' is the first of the rules of Kālidāsa's love. It was based on the conviction that affection binding married persons—

---

1. गृहिणी सचिव: सखी मिथ: प्रिया शिष्या ललिते कलाविधौ ।
करुणाविमुखेन मृत्युना हरता त्वां वद किं न मे हृतम् ॥

Raghu. VIII, 6 ।

2. अर्थो हि कन्या परकीय एव, Shākuntala

though real and valuable—had nothing common with the sentiment of love unless they were separated (Meghadūta). Love was often sought outside marriage. Conditions which governed feudal marriages are sufficient to explain the dogma which sounds so perverse to modern ears. It was the essence of courtly love that should be a thing freely sought and freely given ; it could not be found in the marriage of feudalism (Rāma and Sītā), which was so often a parental arrangement, biding children in the interest of land. Fief marry but men and women love.

This particular conception of love had another characteristic. If the lady stood in a position of superiority towards her lover as uncontested as the position of inferiority in which a wife stood towards husband. Love was, as it were, feudalised ; the lover served his lady as humbly as the vassal served his Lord.[1] He had to keep her identity secret from the world, concealing it under some fictitious name when he praised her in song.[2] He must not only bear himself with the utmost humility towards her, showing infinite patience in the trials to which her caprices and disdains must submit him, but must strive unceasingly to make himself worthy of her. For it was an axim of the theory that every admirable quality had its root in love.

The idea that only by love can man become virtuous or noble informs all the poetry of the troubadours. But moral excellence was not the only virtue grounded in love ; love was also the foundation of literary perfection. The lover must sing as he sighs, and love and poetry become almost interchangeable terms as in Meghadūta also.

A close association of social virtues with love, and the high position given to a woman as their inspiration, are fully reflected both in the conception and in the practice of dramas of Kālidāsa. Love was often platonic in the accepted sense of the term, and in fact had much in common with the true platonic conception of love, in that it made love a source of infinite spiritual possibilities. This conception of platonic love is best exhibited in his lyrics.

It is obvious that a theory which regarded the worship of the lady as next to that of God and conceived her as the mainspring of brave deeds, a creature half male and half woman, must have done something to counteract the prevalent doctrine of women's inferiority.

---

1. अद्यप्रभृत्यवनताङ्गि तवास्मि दासः । Kum. 5.86
2. Māl. 3.72.

The process of placing women on a pedestal had begun, and whatever we may think of the ultimate value of such an elevation, it was at least better than plunging them, as the early Fathers were inclined to do, in the bottomless pit.

Such, then, were the contradictory ideas about women formulated during Kālidāsa's time and handed on as legacy to future generations. On the one hand stood subjection, on the other worship ; both played their part in placing women in the position they occupied in Kālidāsa's age, and in dictating or modifying the conditions of their existence in the subsequent ages. Yet we should be wrong to consider either of these notions as the primary force in determining what the average Kālidāsa, man thought about woman. A social position is never solely created by the retical notions, it was more to the inescapable pressure of facts, the give and take of daily life. And the social position which these facts created in Kālidāsa-society was neither one of superiority nor of inferiority, but one of rough and ready equality. For in daily life man could not do without woman ; he relied on her for the comfort of his home, indeed something like cameraderie is to be found in the writings of Kālidāsa about women.

3.3. Forms of address

Social factors such as age, sex, social stratification affect etc. and differentiate linguistic behaviour of the characters of Kālidāsa. The study of role-relationships and their verbal associates has paid special attention to forms of address. Two aspects are subject to detailed investigation: the use of the familiar and poetic forms of addresses.

Indian writers of Sanskrit grammars have grossly neglected the socio-linguistic dimension of the forms of address in Sanskrit. An attempt will now be made to investigate various social and contextual constraints determining the variant uses of the addresses in Kālidāsa.

In the beginning of the dramas of Kālidāsa, one meets the सूत्रधार, नटी and पारिपार्श्विक. The सूत्रधार addresses his assistant as मारिष while the latter calls him भाव. It is quite in keeping with the convention of address as presented by Bharata (Nātyashāstra 5.156). Bharata advises that individuals of equal status should call one another वयस्य (5.136). He further maintains that the Vidushaka should also be addressed as वयस्य by kings (19.10). We see in the dramas of Kālidāsa that the king दुष्यन्त, पुरूरवा and अग्निमित्र address their respective Vidushakas in the prescribed way. Kālidāsa's female character चित्रलेखा also calls the King as वयस्य. This is somewhat deviation from the Nātyashāstra. Kālidāsa also makes दुष्यन्त call his Vidushaka by his name and this takes the advantage of the option (of Nātyashāstra).

Among female characters of equal status the mode of address is हला. The characters of lower order should be addressed हंजे by female characters of the high rank. Such references to addressing females are not wanting in the plays of Kālidāsa. The birds are addressed as हेले-हेले; while the animals are addressed as हंहो.

According to Bharata, a charioteer should always call the rider आयुष्मन्. In अभिज्ञानशाकुन्तल, दुष्यन्त is always addressed in the same way.

Bharata lays down that the king should be called भर्ता and देव by his subjects. But, as an exception, ascetics are allowed to call him राजन्. Kālidāsa makes use of the same in the drama.

Besides Bharata adds that the ascetics of high rank should be called भगवान्. In अभिज्ञानशाकुन्तल, दुष्यन्त calls मरीचि भगवान् when he visits his hermitage.

On the basis of the Data presented in the next paragraphs we can make the following generalizations about the forms of address in Kālidāsa.

The use of the terms of address is correlated with the social attitudes and status. Lack of switching in the speech of the lower class people, when they are addressing people of the upper class shows that their (lower class people) relationship with the addressee is static. But the addresser from the upper class can switch to other forms of the addresses which shows that if he desires, he can have a dynamic relationship with the one from the lower class.

Then the use of these terms are correlated with familiar relationships. Change, renewal and adjustment of relationships are most frequent in the lover-beloved relationship in the society, which are signalled by frequent switching in the use of the pronominals.

A classified alphabetical list of the forms of address in Kālidāsa is presented below in the following order: (1) Serial No. (2) term of address (3) Source book (4) addresser-addressee (5) Frequency count (6) reference.

3.4. Abusive Words

Kālidāsa has used many phrases which are outside their normal semantic range (with insulting connotations). One third of these abusive terms is associated with the विदूषक (Joker). Joker in Kālidāsa's dramas appears to be a privileged person who can say certain things in a certain way which confers immunity. He is by no means any thing like a taboo-breaker whose polluting act is a real offence to society. He is not exposed to danger. He has a firm hold on his own position in the structure and the disruptive comments which he makes upon it, are in a sense the comments of the social group upon itself. He merely expresses consensus. Safe within the permitted range of attack, he lightens for every one the oppressiveness of social reality, demonstrates its arbitrariness by making light formality in general, and expresses the creative possibility of the situation.

Here is a list of some abusive words of Kālidāsa.

अनात्मज्ञ (कंचुकी—चेटी) 'not knowing self, not knowing her own position that she is a maid-servant and she should obey the king.' Shak.

अनार्य (शकुन्तला—दुष्यन्त) 'not honourable, inferior, doing work unbecoming on Arya' 'आर्याचारविवर्जित-' Shak.

अविनीत (तपस्विनी—बालक सर्वदमन) 'Wanting good manners, having rude behavior' Shak.

असम्बद्धप्रलापिनी (शकुन्तला—प्रियंवदा) 'unconnected talking, uttering unrelated speech' Shak.

आः पुरोभागिनि (शाङ्गरव—शकुन्तला) 'पुरोभागे दोषदर्शिनि (राघवभट्ट) हे दोषमात्रदर्शिनि गुणविमुखि स्वातन्त्र्यं स्वेच्छाचारम् अवलम्बसे किमिति काकुः। पुनः पुनर्दोषमेव त्वं भजसे । पूर्वं बन्धुजनमनावेद्य इम गता इत्येको दोषः अधुना च स्त्री भूत्वा कामाचारं प्रवर्तसे इति द्वितीयः'. In the search after दोष and गुण in the world, we meet with दोष almost at every step. So few are the instances of गुण, that these are found. Thus दोष is पूर्व and गुण is पर. It means '*thou naughty girl.*' It first means पुरोभागः यस्य. One who takes the first share is foremost in sharing, hence, secondarily quarrelsome, naughty, or one who places oneself in the foremost rank, or attaches importance to oneself.

This can only be done by finding fault with others. hence, *fault-finding*'.

कामतन्त्रसचिवः (इरावती—विदूषक) 'secretary of the sex-technology' Mal. 4.33.

कामुक (अङ्गनाः—अग्निवर्ण) 'lustful, voluptuous' Raghu. 19.33

कितव (यक्षिणी—यक्ष, शकुन्तला—दुष्यन्त) 'a cheat, rogue' कितवेन धूर्तेन—राघवः Megh, Shak.

कुणपाशन (दुष्यन्त—मातलि) 'eating dead bodies' कुणपं शवं अश्नाति भक्षयति यस्तत् सम्बुद्धौ । राक्षसः । 'अमेध्यः कुणपाशी च' मनु 12.71. Shak.

कुम्भील(र)क (रक्षक—धीवर) 'a thief' Shak. Vikram, Māl. 'a robber, one who breaks into a house, an alligator, one who drives away an elephant'.

गण्डभेदक (रक्षिणौ—धीवर) 'robber'

ग्रन्थिभेदक (रक्षिणौ—धीवर) 'one who breaks or undoes a knot (for the purpose of stealing money)' Shak.

चोर (पुरूरवा—हंस) 'a thief'

जाल्म (पुरूरवा—केशी) 'a wretch' Vikram. 'जाल्मो बर्बरः, जाल्मोऽसमीक्ष्यकारी'

तिरस्करिणीगर्वित (राजा—मातलि) 'proud of a magical veil rendering the wearer invisible' Shak.

दास्याः पुत्रः (विदूषक—आखेटक) 'the son of a female slave, a low wretch, a miscreant' 'It does not mean that his mother was actually slave, but used merely as an abuse', Shak.

दुरात्मन् (पुरूरवा—राक्षस) 'ill soul' Vikram

दुर्जात (मालविका—बकुलावलिका) 'badly born, miserable, wretched, 'दुर्जातं व्यसने क्लीबे'। Mal.

दुर्विनीते (शकुन्तला—मधुकर) 'badly educated, ill conducted, undisciplined, mean, wicked, obstinate, restive' Shak.

दुष्ट (शकुन्तला—मधुकर) 'naughty' Shak.

दुष्टचेटिका (विदूषक—चेटी) 'bad famale servant' Vikram.

धृष्टः (राजा—मधुकर) 'bold, daring, impudent' Shak.

निर्घृण (शकुन्तला—दुष्यन्त) 'pitiless, heartless, because he has been yet blind to her anguish' Shak.

पाटच्चर (रक्षक—धीवर) 'a thief, a robber'. Shak.

ब्रह्मबन्धु (चेटी—विदूषक / निपुणिका—विदूषक) 'nominal Brahman, an unworthy Brahman, a Brahman who omits his Sandhya—devotion'. Mal. Vikram.

मन्द (विदूषक—आत्मगतं) 'silly, foolish, stupid'. Mal.

मन्दभागिनी (परिव्राजिका—आत्मगतं) 'of ill luck' Mal.

मन्दभाग्या (मालविका—आत्मगतं 'unlucky' Mal.

महाब्राह्मण (गणदास—विदूषक / दुष्यन्त—विदूषक / शार्ङ्गरव—पुरोहित) 'a great Brahman, a priest who officiates at a Shraddha or solemn ceremony in honour of deceased ancestors. The word महत् when prefixed to such words as ब्राह्मण, वैद्य etc. implies निन्दा or censore, i.e. absence of the real qualities. It is a slightly taunting word too. It is a term sufficiently flattering to the simple minded विदूषक, who is unable to see irony in it.'' Mal. Shak.

मूढ (पुरूरवा—विदूषक) 'stupid, foolish' Vikram. Mal.

मूर्ख (पुरूरवा— विदूषक) 'foolish'. Vik.

मृत्पिण्डबुद्धि (विदूषक—आत्मगतं) 'a person who thinks to officiate solemn-ceremony in honour of deceased ancestors'. Shak.

विहगाधम (राजा—गिद्ध) 'a bad bird' Vik.

वैधेय: (सेनापति—विदूषक) 'a fool, a block head, idiot, one who has yet to learn what the shastras say' Shak. Vik.

शठ (इरावती—अग्निमित्र) 'Wicked, false lover, one who pretends affection for one female while his heart is fixed on another.' Mal.

हताश: (निपुणिका—विदूषक) 'whose hopes are destroyed, desperate, helpless' Mal.

हताशा (निपुणिका—इरावती) 'desperate' Mal.

3.5. The Art of Naming

In ancient years students of Kālidāsa have noticed many examples of suggestive naming. Scholarly comments run all the ways from

Anandavardhan's brief generalization to Kshemendra's lengthy theory on Kālidāsa's presentation or the popular etymology of the names. The attention given to the 'etymologies presented by Kālidāsa' arouses careful readers to become increasingly aware that Kālidāsa is naming artistic in his, let us examine. The extent to which he carried symbolic naming and the way this device functions in his works.

There are many examples of suggestive naming in Kālidāsa. He matched names to characters.

From the descriptions of the names several concepts emerge which are useful in analyzing the meaning of the names used in the works of Kālidāsa. The most important concept that Kālidāsa chose names, in some cases, because they were amusing लातव्य in some cases because they had meaning in terms of character—चित्रलेखा, मालविका, कौमुदिका, समाहितिका, जयसेना, तरलिका, मदनिका, माधविका, चतुरिका, सानुमती, सर्वदमन, धनमित्र, इयामल, सूचक, वातायन etc.; in some cases because they had none———सहजन्या, वाहतक, यज्ञसेन, भद्रसेन, माटव्य, सोमरात, हारीत, जानुक, and in other cases because he felt attracted to the name for no discrete reason. Consequently, not all the names in his works will have meaning and certainly some will have some private association. They will remain secret but availability for interpretation.

From the above discussion, it is plain that Kālidāsa considered as an important part of his writing and was aware that in theory at least, the suggestive name could contribute meaning without destroying realism. Though most of the names for which any significance can be found are taken from ordinary words chosen for their suggestive powers. Some can be grouped together because they have a common source of meaning. For example, many names come from Ramayana, Mahabharata and puranic literature ; others come from history and myth. But the particular group, however, is made up of names that do not lend themselves to any neat category but run the whole gamut of Kālidāsa's image making powers. Of this latter group, some are easy to detect, other are more subtle and can be convincingly discussed only in terms of their use within a particular drama.

In drawing names from the world of nature Kālidāsa could expect the association raised in the minds of readers to be fairly uniform. For a nice, fresh, innocent but rather common variety of Indian girl, he chose बकुलावलिका. Like the field-flower she has grown up uncultivated but quite lovely and natural. Another young girl निपुणिका carries an image of cleverness. The distinction Kālidāsa makes between the two is important. In the same way the distinction between two innocent pupils—गालव and पल्लव is also very fascinating.

Somewhat unflattering images are suggested by the characterization of various birds हंसपदिका and शकुन्तला are the beloveds of दुष्यन्त with a changed story. परमृतिका and मधुकरिका are the maidens. The names suggest that these are sensitive young women who rise above conventional society.

A second source of suggestive naming is history and myth. The names of several characters have already received the attention of the historians—अग्निमित्र, पुष्यमित्र, वसुमित्र, यज्ञसेन, माधवसेन, आयुष, भरत, पुरूरवा, दुष्यन्त, इरावती, प्रियम्वदा, अनसूया, गौतमी, शकुन्तला, उर्वशी, रम्भा, and मेनका. The inspiration for heroines comes from myth rather than history.

Other mythological names are of little assistance in unlocking meaning, the parallels being very general at best.

The third group of purposeful names is made up mainly of connotative words, although the meanings of many of these are highly conjectural—वसुलक्ष्मी, and वसुमती etc.

Other names, though less glaringly suggestive than those listed above, can be seen to function purposefully. Kālidāsa employs names in a variety of ways to add to the humour. Often they are a means by which he sharpens his readers awareness of social class or profession—सुव्रता, सूचक, माणवक, गणदास, घनमित्र and लातव्य etc. are the names depicting social status.

The question why Kālidāsa used symbolic and suggestive names so extensively does not level itself to an easy answer. Partly because their function does not always seem to be the same. Frequently they are so more than an expression of humorous word-play and are bestowed on such minor character as to seem hardly worth the effort. At other times, however, the names are so closely related to theme and imagery that all the three seem to rise from the same impulse.

3.6. Non-verbal Communication among the Characters of Kālidāsa

The characters of Kālidāsa speak with their vocal organs, but they converse with their entire bodies ; conversation consists of more than a simple interchange of spoken words. The term 'non-verbal communication', as it is currently employed, is most frequently used to refer to all of the ways in which communication is effected between characters when in each other's presence, by means other than words. It refers to communicational functioning of bodily activity, gesture, facial expression and orientation, posture and spacing, touch and smell, and of those aspects of utterance that can be considered apart from the referential content of what is said. Studies of non-verbal communication of Kālidāsa are usually concerned with the part these aspects of behaviour play in establishing and maintaining interaction and interpersonal relations between the characters. Anyone with a professional interest in dramatic language is likely, sooner or later, to have to take an interest in non-verbal communication too.

Dramas were written by Kālidāsa in the specific intention of staging them.[1] The author himself was giving stage direction in his works to guide actors in the action of particular scenes. We find 1156 such stage directions in the works of Kālidāsa ; 507 in Shākuntala, 332 in Vikramōrvashīya and 327 in Mālavikāgnimitra. Some of them are already found on dramaturgy, while others indicate the deep understanding and insight of the art of acting of Kālidāsa.

There are two types of languages in the dramas. One is 'Sarvashrāvya' and the other is 'ashrāvya' or 'ātmagata'. 'Ātmagata' are such utterances during which characters on the stage are supposed to act as if they are not hearing there, though they are heard by the whole of the audience. There is one more interesting type which is called "niyatashrāvya" heard by a limited set of characters in the stage, while others present at the same time and spot have to pretend as if they have not heard. 'Niyatashrāvya' is of two types : (1) *apavārita* and (2) *janāntika*. 'Ākāshabhāshita' and 'Karṇe' are other well known stage directions.

The gestural expressions of 'giving skin' and 'getting skin' are very common in the dramas. These gestures of giving and getting skill may be considered as kinemes. They derive their meaning from the analysis of the entire range of components involved in a communicative act—sender, receiver, channel, code, setting etc. The *kinemes* of giving and getting skin can be combined with facial expressions (such as 'smita', 'vismaya', 'āvega' 'asūya', 'vrīḍā' and

1. आपरितोषाद् विदुषाम् etc. Shak.

'harsha' etc.) to produce *kinemorphs.* The variations within each of the kinemes represent subtle, individual *allokines* of giving skin.

Here we may analyse the regular kinemes of giving and getting skin. The salutation to the sages is treated as imparting great benefit (Shāk. v.) Shākuntā with her child postrates (Shāk. VII) herself before the sacred feet of the divine parents. These gestures are tools used by individuals for their own specific needs, and there are as many varieties and styles of doing these simple acts as there are individual personalities. Shākuntala (5) illustrates the palm-to-palm kineme of giving cup his hand slightly or hold it straight out. Thus we can consider four major kinemes of giving and getting skin in Kālidāsa : (1) greeting skin (2) parting skin (3) complementary skin, and (4) agreement skin. In addition four major means of execution may be considered : (a) on the sly (b) emphatic (c) superlative, and (d) regular.

Standing stances are also communicative in the Sanskrit dramas. Vikrama. (1) illustrates the use of the lowered-shoulder kineme which is common in the stances and walks of most males. Māla. (4) illustrates the use of shoulder kineme in dancing.

There are several ways a female may indicate to a man that she is interested in him by the way he walks. One basic kind of Jaunt consisting of a back-and forth hip-swinging movement is also found. What is unique in the characters is the overall rhythm of the walk, as well as the forward-and-backward motion of the shoulders which creates movement in the breast area. This kind of walk, which involves movements of many parts of the body is referred to as "shaking it up".

Shāk. (3) is illustrative of another use of gestures in the Sanskrit dramas. This particular interaction occurred spontaneously in a social situation involving the introduction of two people.

The oriental handshake or greeting can be divided into three components in a given sequence. They are :

1. grasping each other's hands, interpreted as meaning *strength ;*

2. mutual grasping of hands, meaning *solidarity*;

3. placing hands on shoulders with as light amount of pressure, indicating *comradeship.*

Other aspects of nonverbal communication are hair and clothing. The hairstyle is a symbol of pride in self and heritage. Just as clothes and hair consciously affirm oriental people's strength and unity of purpose for the achievement of control of their lives and destinies, so do the selected kinesic forms of nonverbal communication depicted here act on a deeper level of awareness.

Dependent audible elements which are extremely varied, might all be put together under another popular term, tones of voice. They are produced by variations from the sociolinguistic norm in features of voice dynamics—laughter, yawning, distance, anger, fear, pleasure and shyness etc.

A cursory reading of the Sanskrit dramas of Kālidāsa shows that if we were to rely exclusively on what words those characters say, a good part of the total message of Kālidāsa would be simply known. One can conclude from the aforegoing the creation, transmission, and perception of the people in the literary world of Kālidāsa is a process based on the author's own exclusive circumstance in the real world, at one end, and the individual reader's own exclusive circumstance, also in the real world, at the other; each of them occurring in a specific spatial and temporal situation.

From the discussion of how nonverbal communication in literature reveals the semiotic process which in turn shows the author-character-reader relationship, and of how the character's repertoires affect the literary text itself, we could conclude that the use of those repertoires is a necessary inherent to Kālidāsa.

3.7. Kinship

The words revealing the kinship usage in the works of Kālidāsa, show two types of arrangements of the term, one for the members of the family by birth and the other for the members of the family by marriage. In each set, there are distinct terms for three generations of the "ego".

The words for the ego's generations are : bhrātṛ (i.e. brother) and bhaginī (i.e., the sister). The word 'bhrātṛ' is used in Vedic hymns, but 'bhaginī' is not found in the Vedic text. For brother, Kālidāsa has used three words—'bhrātṛ', 'agraja' and 'anuja', Bhrātṛ denotes the meaning of the 'brother'. It can be used for elder brother as well as for the younger brother also, while 'agraja' is used for the elder brother and 'anuja' is used for the younger one specifically. One more term can be seen that is "Saudarya", but it is not so common as 'bhrātṛ'.

'Bhaginī' (sister) is also used for both the elder as well as younger sister. To denote the meaning of younger sister the adjective 'Kanist' is used.

The words for the ego's parents' generation are : 'pitṛ', 'tāta' for father and "mātṛ', 'ambā' for mother. The dual form of the 'pitṛ' means 'the parents' (i.e., mother and father both) ; while the plural form of 'pitṛ' means 'the dead ancestors', especially those who are supposed to receive food offered by them.

The terms for the younger generation of the ego are "Sūnu", "putra", "Vatsa" "Suta" for son ; and "duhitṛ", "Kanyā", "putrī", "tanujā", "Sutā", "Vatsā" for daughter. The terms "putra" and "vatsa" are also used for any boy or younger one i.e., any elderly person may call his younger associate by the term "vatsa" or "putra", besides his own son ; viz., Mālatī calls Dushyanta by the term 'vatsa'.

The son of the son is called "pautra". Rarely the term 'dauhitra' is used for the daughter's son.

Ego's female offspring is known by the terms "duhitṛ", "kanyā", "putrī", "tanujā", "suta" etc. "vatsā" is common term of address for any girl. "Kanyā" specially denotes the meaning of a "virgin girl".

Ego's kin by marriage are known as "pati or "bhartā" (i.e., husband) and "patnī" and "bhāryā" (i.e. wife). There are various terms for both, which Kālidāsa has used. The mode of address by a wife for husband is "āryaputra" (the son of the honoured one). The husband is always so addressed by the wife. While using this orthodox kinship term for husband, Kālidāsa has also marshalled many poetic and aesthetic terms like 'priya', 'ananga', 'ratipaṇḍita', 'Saumya', 'mādhava', 'Kusumāyudha' and 'smara' etc.

Before going into deep into the matter related to kinship usage, it is desirable to present the chart, that will help to elaborate the hypothesis.

The whole concept of kinship and family was social and legal in Kālidāsa. Instead of starting the description of a family from 'father and mother', it would be better to start from the 'husband-wife' relationship as for as data in Kālidāsa are concerned. A girl becomes a wife of a person by a public ritual known as "vivāha".

The word 'gṛhapatnī' needs some clarification. 'Gṛha patnī' was considered to be the elder-son's wife, and also the chief amongst the other wives, as our ancient Indian society was a

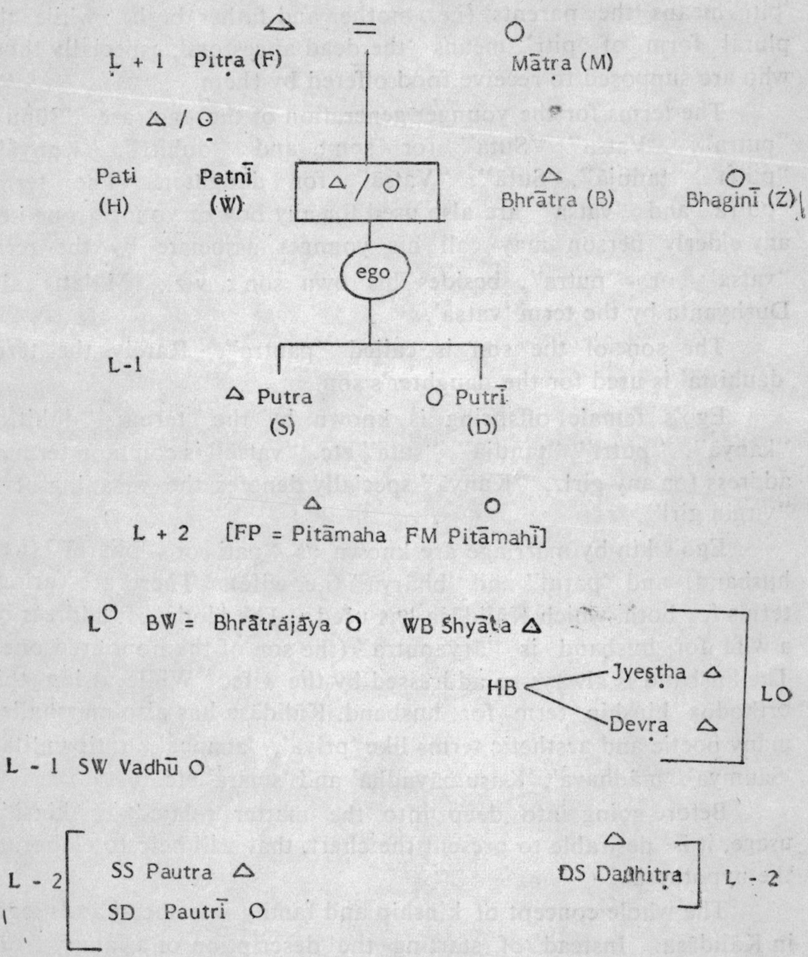
L + 1 Pitṛa (F)
Mātra (M)
Pati (H)
Patnī (W)
Bhrātra (B)
Bhaginī (Z)
ego
L-1
Putra (S)
Putrī (D)
L + 2 [FP = Pitāmaha FM Pitāmahī]
L° BW = Bhrātrájāya
WB Shyāta
HB
Jyeṣṭha
Devra
LO
L - 1 SW Vadhū
L - 2
SS Pautra
SD Pautrī
DS Dauhitra
L - 2

polygamous. Naturally, 'duhitṛ' (daughters) were blessed to obtain the respected seat of 'gṛha-patnī, as stated in Ṛgveda also. Shakuntalā was blessed by Kaṇva for the same fate.

If we analyse the dramas of Kālidāsa we find that love-marriages (gandharva vivāha) was prevalent in his time which was the arranged marriage between the lovers without any ritual. None of the relative's or public consent is involved, though it is apparent that the norms of the society never approved such type of marriage, that is why Kālidāsa had always punished his characters for observing the free mentality about their affairs by means of creating curse-technique.

To conclude, we may say that 'patnī', 'bhāryā' or dārā' is the nearest associate of ego.

Kin of the wife by marriage is known by the term 'pati' or 'bhartṛ' in Sanskrit literature. He is the centre of the family as well as of kinship organization. In other words we can say the ego is the head of the family of his generation. Obviously, the elder generation's head would be the father of the ego. Apparently, he has parents, grand parents, wife, brothers, sisters, aunts and uncles, cousins and children. This hierarchy can be easily assessed through an illustrated chart given on page next.

In Sanskrit literature as well as in Kālidāsa, we can observe the same hierarchy of a patriarchal family.

Ego's wife's brother (Shyālaka) was supposed to be an eminent person in the king's court. In Shākuntala also 'Shyālaka' played an important role in capturing the fisherman along with Dushyanta's ring.

The kinship in our ancient Indian society and culture can be classified in an orderly manner keeping the levels of relation in view. To have a rational approach, they can be classified as first order, second order and third order relations.

First order relations are those relations which exist in the basic unit of a family. In other words, they are direct relations, and may be consanguries or Affines—e.g., Father-son, Brother-sister, Husband-wife.

Second order relations are such relations where a person is essentially involved in between to establish relation such as Father's sister, Mother's father, Brother's wife etc.

Third order relations are relatively distant relations—in comparison to first and second order relations, where two persons are

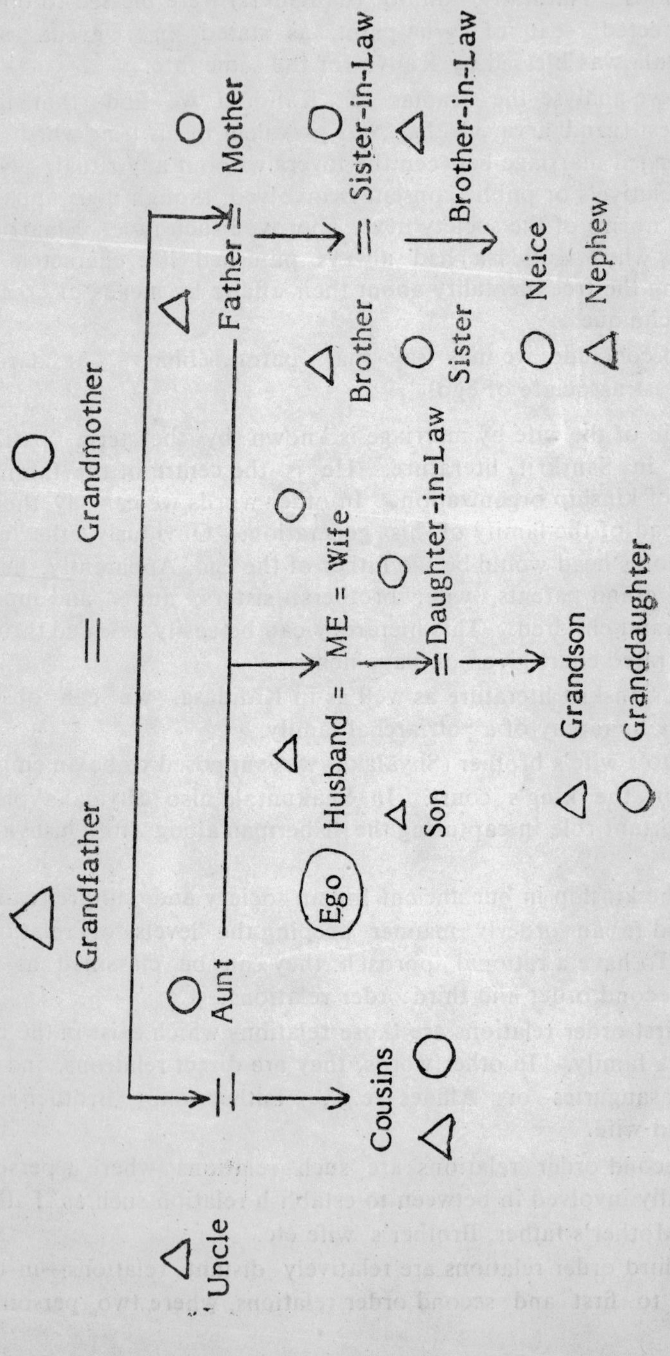

Grandfather
Grandmother
Uncle
Aunt
Father
Mother
Cousins
Ego
Husband = ME = Wife
Brother
Sister-in-Law
Sister
Brother-in-Law
Son
Daughter-in-Law
Neice
Nephew
Grandson
Granddaughter

essentially needed to establish the relation—for instance, Father's brother's son, Brother's wife's father, Mother's brother's wife etc.

In nutshell we can say that the first strata or order of relation is direct relation which does not need any link, second order needs one link and third order needs two links. The following tables present the whole kinship organization which was existing in ancient Indian society.

Table No. 1.		**First Order Relations**
L+1	Pitṛ (F)	Matṛ (M)
LO	Pati (H)	Patnī (W)
	Bhrātṛ (B)	Bhaginī (Z)
L−1	Putra (S)	Putri (D)

Table No. 2		**Second Order relations**
L+2	Pitāmaha (FF)	Mātāmaha (FM)
	Pitṛvya (FB)	Mātula (MB)
		Matṛ svasa (MZ)
	WF	
	svasura	
	HF	
	WM	
	svaśrū	
	HM	
LO	Bhrātṛjāya (BW)	Shyāla (WB)
		Shyalika (WZ)
L—1	Vadhū (SW)	
L—2	Pautra (SS)	Pautrī (SD)

Table No. 3		**Third order relations**
L+3	Prapitāmaha (FFF)	
	Pramātāmaha (FFM)	

The strata of kinship organization kept the society intact through ages. Still these strata are prevailing in the society. Thus, the kinship controls rules and regulations regarding marriage character and religion.

To conclude, the kinship system can by treated as a 'proto' system, and the basic meaning of the kinship organization is 'father', (i.e. father is prototype) and the other meanings are derived from this by applying any of the three equivalence rules:

A—a man's sister is equivalent to his mother.

B—sibling of the same sex are equivalent to each other.

C—half-sibling are equivalent to full siblings. This can be well understood by a table.

Rule	**Meaning**
Prototype	Father
B. Sibling=sibling	Father's brother
C. Half-sibling=full	Father's father's son
B. Sibling=sibling	Father's father's brother's son
C. Half sibling=full	Father's father's mother's son's son
A. Sister=mother	Father's father's sister's son's son

This discovery opens the possibility that if we compare the prototype meanings of kinship terminology from different languages we shall find that there are relatively few variations on a few very general patterns, though we may expect difference in the rules of derivation. The difference in those rules cannot be dismissed as unimportant, of course, because they can have dramatic and far reaching consequences, but at least we seem to have restricted the kinds of differences between kinship terminologies in different languages and no longer see them as evidence for extreme relativity.

3.8. Folk-etymology

It is interesting to note that numerous instances of Folk-etymology (लोक निरुक्ति) are found in Sanskrit literature beginning from the Vedic time down to the end of classical period. These instances are sometimes recorded by Sanskrit grammarians under the heading पृषोदरादि. Some of the commentators of Sanskrit lexicography have tried to explain them not directly by applying the rules of Sanskrit grammars, but by turning and twisting the words according to their desires.

The word 'etymology' (Skt. निरुक्ति) means 'the true account and analysis of a word.' It comes from the Greek word 'etumos' which means 'true' and 'logos' which means 'word.' Therefore by joining the two words, it means 'that part of philology which explains the origin and derivation of a word, with a view to ascertain their radical or primary significance.'

Folk-etymology or False-etymology is the replacement of an unknown word by a more familiar one. "It is the result of popular instinct," say Graff (Language and Languages) "for associating together words which resemble each other in sound and perhaps in meaning although there is no historical relationship between them."

Knowledge of lexicons and right use of words is essential for equipment of a poet according to all Sanskrit rhetoricians. Right knowledge of their origin ; and the science of etymology is one which deals with the origin of words in a way. Naturally poets must have turned to the NIRUKTA to complete their poetic equipment. It will be interesting to observe how poets turned the science of NIRUKTA to their poetic use.

In Kālidāsian literature we often meet etymological explanation of words, which are mostly meaningless, viewed from the standpoint of modern scientific etymological analysis of Indo-Aryan comparative Philology. Most of them are more or less a kind of wort-spiel, which connect a given word arbitrarily with a similar verb-root which has originally no connection with it. But this approach to the word had a ritual, rather than a linguistic significance, because the standpoint of Kālidāsa is completely the object which the word indicates ; and thus the analysis of a word means nothing to him but that of the object. The full understanding of the word by means of an etymological device was believed by him to lead to the full insight into the object which the word indicated. The name and its object, that is the name-possessor, are magically and ritually connected, with each other, and Kālidāsa was not amusing himself but serious in analysing the word, seeing this attempt as a way to approach the essence of the thing. As for example, Kālidāsa suggests the following explanation of the name of उमा and अपर्णा in his Kumārasambhava :

तां पार्वतीत्याभिजनेन नाम्ना
बन्धुप्रियां बन्धुजनो जुहाव ।
उमेति मात्रा तपसो निषिद्धा
पश्चादुमाख्यां सुमुखी जगाम ।। (1.26)

i.e., "The body of her relatives called her, to whom her relatives were so dear पार्वती, a name derived from the family of her father. Subsequently, when her mother dissuaded her from her resolve to practise penance by saying उ मा (oh ! no) the lovely faced girl was thence forward known by the name of उमा."

स्वयं विशीर्णद्रुमपर्णवृत्तिता
परा हि काष्ठा तपसस्तया पुनः ।
तदप्यपाकीर्णमतः प्रियंवदां
वदन्त्यपर्णेति च तां पुराविदः ।।

i.e. "To subsist on leaves of trees that drop withered of their own accord is the utmost height that penance can reach; she, however, left off even that ; this is the reason why people versed in ancient lore call that sweet-tongued girl अपर्णा."

In Kālidāsian age the Brahminical tradition still preserves and we find a number of etymological analysis of personal names often they are accompanied by legendary stories which recount the origin of those names and the history of how they became so named.

At any rate it should be here noted that the etymological study reveals to us the historical background of the word most scientifically, the folk-etymological explanations found in the works of Kālidāsa sometimes enable us to discern what sort of concrete ideas the poet had about the given concept, the names of which he attempted to analyse by bio-etymological device.

To prepare an exhaustive list of these folk-etymological explanations found in Kālidāsa requires vast time and space, so we limit our attention only to some broad classifications Kālidāsa offers false-etymologies on the following words : अगस्त्य, अहीनगु:, इन्दुमती, ककुत्स्थ, कौसल्य, क्षेमधन्वा, गोप्रतरकल्प, तपन:, तमसा, दशरथ, ध्रुवसन्धि, नन्दिनी, परन्तप, प्रतीप, मनु, रघु, राजा, राम, लोकालोक, विराध, विश्वसह, शत्रुघ्न, शूर्पणखा, सुदक्षिणा, सुदर्शन, हरिणी, हेमाङ्गद, उन्नाभ, दिलीप, दूषण, नभ, निषध, पारियात्र, पुण्डरीक, मेघनाद, हिरण्यनाभ, नल, पुष्य, अज, कुशलव, व्युषिताश्व, देवानीक, नर्मदा, मधुरा, वज्र, शिल:, सुतीक्ष्ण, सुमित्रा, पारिजात, पुष्पक, वसिष्ठ, भरषि, कवि, क्षत्र, चन्द्र, दुर्गा, पादप, पिता, रवि, विष्णु, सारस, सुपर्ण, (रघुवंश), गन्धमादन, पार्वती, मैना, सती, उच्चै:श्रवा, तारक, अपर्णा, उमा, गौरीशिखर, त्रिविक्रम, पत्नी, हार (कुमारसम्भव), प्रियंवदा, भरत, सर्वदमन, परभृतिका, मधुकरिका, सखी, (शाकुन्तल), ध्रुवसिद्धि, धारिणी, बकुलावलिका (मालविकाग्निमित्र), आयु, उर्वशी, सङ्गमनीय (विक्रमोर्वशीय), अलका, आम्रकूट, गन्धवती, गम्भीरा, रामगिरि, and विशाला (मेघदूत).

Now from all the material given above it will become clear that the bulk of Kālidāsa's etymologies is to be found in the Raghuvaṁsha, while the Kumārasambhava comes next. In Shākuntala we come across only sex etymologies. The Meghadūta also contains sex. Mālavikāgnimitra and Vikramorvashiya share equal, while Ṛtusaṁhār contains no etymology.

It seems that Kālidāsa uses bio-etymologies to pay significant compliment to his heroes and heroines. In the Canchsian it must be said that Kālidāsa never uses etymologies for their own sake nor in order to show off his scholarship. After all Kālidāsa wrote poetry and not a treatise on the science of etymology.

3.9. Semantic Change

Language, like anything else that depends upon human beings, changes considerably with the passage of time. One result of this is that when we read the literature of several hundred years ago we are likely to be misled by words that have changed their meaning since the book was written ; and sometimes much more recent writing contains a few words to which this has happened. Indeed, changes in the meaning, specially the associations, of words are sometimes so rapid that they contribute difficulties of understanding between two generations.

This is one reason why the classical Sanskrit literature, especially the works of Kālidāsa, often have to be printed with explanatory notes ; unfortunately the explanatory notes often look very uninteresting and arouse suspicions that the book is going to be dull.

A person who is able to read classical Sanskrit is not likely to be misled by these historical changes, since she language is so unlike Modern Sanskrit that he knows he has to look in the dictionary very frequently. A person reading Kālidāsa's works often misunderstands because he is not looking for changes in meaning. The misleading word is the one that looks the same as the one we are used to and that, in the context, could reasonably mean what we at first sight suppose.

A comparative study, of pre-Kālidāsian words and Kālidāsian words or Kālidāsian and Hindi vocabularies reveals a number of interesting facts as regards words and their meanings. On account of changed conditions the meaning has displaced, or extended; or specialized.

(*a*) *Displacement of meaning*

1. अकाल The word अकाल in CDK means 'Wrong, inauspicious or unreasonable time, not proper time'. In Hindi अकाल means 'famine.'
2. अंगार In CDK the word अंगार is used in the sense of 'Charcoal.' In Hindi this word is used in the sense of 'burning charcoal.'

3. अनुशासन means 'advice, persuasion, instruction, laying down rules, or percepts.' In Hindi this word is used in the sense of 'discipline'.
4. अवकाश means 'occasion' opportunity; for example, ताते चापद्वितीये वहति रणधुरां को भयस्यावकाश: (Venisamhara 3.5). It also means 'place, space, room'. e.g. अवकाशो विविक्तोऽयं समागमे (Rāmāyana). It is also used in the sense of 'admission, access, entrance', as छाया शुद्धे तु दर्पणतले शुद्धावकाशा (Shak. 7.32). In Hindi this is used in the sense of 'spare time, holiday, vacation, leave, retirement.'
5. आयु: In CDK the word आयु means 'life, duration of life' e.g. दीर्घायुर्भव. In Hindi it is used in the sense of 'age.'
6. आलोक The word आलोक means दृष्टि in Sanskrit dictionaries, while CDK records it in the meaning of जयशब्द: Mallinātha also supports this : आलोको जयशब्द: स्यात् इति विश्व: । In this sense this word is used in Raghuvaṁsha (2.9).

   विसृष्टपार्श्वानुचरस्य तस्य
   पार्श्वद्रुमा: पाशभृतासमस्य ।
   उदीरयामासुरिवोन्मदाना
   मालोकशब्दं वयसां विरावै: ॥

   Some time Kālidāsa uses this word in the sense of light which is being sustained in Hindi :

   मेघालोके भवति सुखिनो
   ऽप्यन्यथावृत्तिचेत: । (Megha. 1.3)
7. औष्म, औष्म is used in the sense of सन्ताप or उष्ण in pre-CDK. Kālidāsa used it in the sense of grief :

   पूर्वराजवियोगौष्मं
   कृत्स्नस्य जगतो हृतम् (Raghu. 17.33)
8. कठिन The word कठिन is used in the sense of hard, e.g.,

   कठिनविषमामेकवेणीं सारयन्तीम् (Megh. 92)

   This word also means hard hearted, cruel, restless; e.g.

   न विदीर्ये कठिना: खलु स्त्रिय: (Kum.)

In Hindi this word is used in the sense of 'difficulty'.

9. कुलिश In Amarakosha कुलिश means शतकोटि, while Kālidāsa used it in the sense of कोटि :
तत्रावश्यं वलयकुलिशोद्‌घट्टनोद्‌गीर्णतोयं (Megh.)

10. क्रिया In pre-CDK क्रिया means creation or work. CDK defines it as साहित्यिक सृष्टि, e.g.,
क्रियामिमां कालिदासस्य (Vik. 1.2)

11. चूर्ण In CDK चूर्ण means 'dust or powder of any thing', e.g. भवति विफलप्रेरणाचूर्णमुष्टिः (Megh. 68). The tadbhava form चूरा is used in Hindi in this very sense. The word चूर्ण means 'a saltish preparation which is considered conductive of digestion.'

12. तस्कर in CDK means 'a thief or robber in general sense.' In Hindi the sense of this word has been narrowed and it is now used for 'a smuggler' only.

13. दुर्दिन is मेघाच्छन्नदिन (cloudy day) in pre-CDK, but in CDK it is धारासम्पातवर्षण (raining cats and dogs). In Hindi it is used in the sense of 'hard days.'

14. पराग is पुष्परज in Sanskrit dictionaries, but in CDK it is धूलि (dust). In Hindi again it has retained the old meaning.

प्रतापोऽग्रे ततः शब्दः
परागस्तदनन्तरम् (Raghu. 4.30)

15. परामर्श In CDK the word is used in the sense of (a) seizing (b) bending (c) violence (d) hindrance, e.g., तपःपरामर्शविवृद्धमन्योः (Kum.), (e) recollection. In Hindi this word used in the sense of 'consultation'.

16. प्रचार means 'going forth, walking about, wandering.' It also means 'appearance, coming in the manifestation, currency, prevalence.' It is used also in the sense of 'conduct, behaviour, custom, usage.' This very sense has developed in Hindi as 'propnganda' convassing etc.'

17. प्रस्ताव means 'beginning, commencement, introduction'. The same sense is still presented in the word प्रस्तावना which is equally used in CDK as well as in Hindi. It also means 'mention, allusion, reference', e.g., नाममात्रप्रस्तावः

(Shak. 7.) It also means 'an occasion, opportunity, fit or proper time', e.g., त्वरा प्रस्तावोऽयं न खलु परिहासस्य. Moreover, it is used in the sense of 'the occasion of discourse, subject, topic'. In Hindi this word is used in two different senses: (1) proposal and (2) essay.

18. बर्ह In Sanskrit dictionaries this word is found in the sense of 'peacock's tail' (मयूरपिच्छ), but Kālidāsa uses it in the sense of कुसुमकिसलय :

विलासिनीविभ्रमदन्तपत्र—
मापाण्डुरं केतकबर्हमन्यः । (Raghu. 6.74)

19. श्रेणी The meanings of this word in CDK are 'a line, series, group, flock, multitude.' In Hindi this word is used in the sanse of 'a class of students.'

(b) *Extension of meaning*

20. अवतार means 'appearance of any deity upon earth, descent' in Sankrit dictionaries, while Kālidāsa used it in the sense of 'appearance of any thing', e.g.,

धर्मार्थकाममोक्षाणामवतार इवाङ्कभाक् (Raghu. 10.84)

In Hindi it retains pre-Kālidāsian meaning.

21. अवधि is 'time' for Kālidāsa, but it is 'period' in other Skt. writers and Hindi :

मनोज्ञगन्धं सहकारभङ्ग—
पुराणसीधुं नवपाटलं च ।
सम्बध्नता कामिजनेषु दोषाः
सर्वे निदाघावधिना प्रमृष्टाः ॥

22. ओषधि The Word ओषधि in CDK generally means 'a hurb, a plant, a medical plant or drug.' In Hindi the word ओषधि is used in a wider sense. It includes not only the herbs or medical plants, but all sorts of medicines.

23. आरोप In Kālidāsa the word आरोप means 'attributing the nature and properties of one thing to another, arising'. It also means super-imposition. In Hindi the word आरोप means 'a charge against any person, blame'.

24. उदास means 'one who sits with his mouth raised up; hence, 'indifferent, apathetic, unconcerned to the world'. It also means 'a stoic philosopher'. In Hindi this word is used in the degenerated sense 'worried.'

25. उद्योग means 'effort, exertion, work, duty, diligence, etc. In Hindi this word has come to mean 'industry, branch of manufacture'.

26. कीर्त्तन in CDK means 'telling, repeating, narrating etc. The word is derived from the root कीर्त्त् which means 'to recite, repeat, mention etc'. In Hindi this word means 'a peculiar way of reciting the sacred names of God or gods'.

27. ग्लानि in CDK means 'exhaustion, langour, fatigue'; e.g., अङ्गग्लानिं सुरतजनिताम् (Megh.). It also means 'decay'. In Hindi this word has come to mean 'disgust, aversion, contempt'.

28. समाधि in CDK means (a) composing (b) attention (c) completion (d) concentration of thoughts (e) eighth and last stage of yoga : यदा फलं पूर्वतपः समाधिना (Kum. 5.18) (f) rule: सा भूधराणामधिपेन तस्यां
समाधिमत्यामुदपादि भव्या (Kum. 1.22)

In Hindi the yogic meaning is prevalent.

(c) *Specialization of meaning*

29. अन्तर is used in CDK in many senses. First, it means 'related, intimate, dear', e.g. अयमन्यतरो मे, secondly, it means 'exterior, situated outside' Thirdly, it is used in the sense of 'difference', e.g., तव च मम च समुद्रपल्वलयोरिवान्तरम् (Mal.). Fourthly, it is used in the sense of 'another, other'. In Hindi the word is used in the sense of difference.

30. अपवाद in CDK means 'censuring, reproach, blame', e.g., लोकापवादो बलवान् मतो मे (Raghu. 16.40). It is also used, though very rarely, in the sense of 'an exception'. In Hindi the latter sense has been prominent while the former has been abandoned.

31. अभियोग in CDK means 'devotion, energetic effort, exertion', e.g. सन्तः स्वयं परहितेषु कृताभियोगाः It is also used in the sense of 'devotion to learn some thing,' e.g, कस्यां कलायामभियोगो भवत्याः. It also means 'learned, scholarship'. It is also, though rarely, used in the sense of 'a charge, accusation'. This way sense has become prominent in Hindi abondoning all the other altogether.

32. आतङ्क has three senses (1) disease, sickness of the body (2) pain affliction (of the mind), anguish, agony, and (3) fear, apprehension, fright, terror. In Hindi the first two senses are no longer in use while the third one only survives.

33. आदर्श means 'a mirror, a looking glass'. It also means 'the original manuscript from which a copy is taken, model; e.g. आदर्शः शिक्षितानाम्. In Hindi this word is used in the sense of 'model'.

34. आशा The word आशा in CDK means 'hope, expectation, prospect'. It is also used in the sense of 'false hope or expectation'. Moreover, it means space, region, quarter of the compass, direction. In Hindi this word is used only in the sense of 'hope, expectation, prospect.'

35. कवि The word कवि in CDK means 'a wiseman, a thinker, a sage.' The word also means 'a poet,' e.g. मन्दः कवियशः प्रार्थी (Raghu. 1.3). In Hindi the former sense has altogether gone, while the latter only has been retained.

36. कुशेशय means 'lotus' in pre-CDK, while it means 'red lotus' in Kālidāsa :

सहस्रपत्रं कमलं शतपत्रं कुशेशयम् (Amarakosha)
कुशेशयाताम्रतलेन कश्चि-
त्करेणरेखाध्वजलांछनेन (Raghu. 6.18)

37. कौतुक The word generally means 'festival' in Sanskrit dictionaries. Kālidāsa uses it in the sense of 'marriage-festival' :

कन्यकातनयकौतुकक्रियाम् (Raghu. 11.53)

In another context Kālidāsa uses it in the sense of हस्तसूत्र.

38. घृणा The word घृणा in Kālidāsa means 'compassion, pity, tenderness'. This word is also used in the sense of 'disgust; aversion, contempt.' In Hindi only the last sense has been retained.

39. क्षण The word क्षण in CDK means 'an instant, moment'. It also means 'leisure' अहमपि क्षणलब्धः स्वगेहं गच्छामि (Mal. 1) In Hindi only the first sense has been retained.

40. प्रजा: The word प्रजा in Kālidāsa means 'procreation, generation, propagation, birth production'. It is also used in the sense of 'offspring, progeny, issue, children, brood (of animals), e.g. प्रजार्थव्रतकर्षिताङ्गः (Raghu. 2.73). It also means 'subject, people, mankind,' e.g. ननन्दुः सप्रजाः प्रजाः (Raghu). In the last two examples the word has been used in both the senses. In Hindi only the latter sense has been retained.

41. प्रतिष्ठाः The word प्रतिष्ठा is used in a large number of senses in Kālidāsa. One sense is resting, remaining, situation, position,' e.g. अपौरुषेय प्रतिष्ठाम् (Mal. I). The other sense is 'a house, residence, home, habitation (Raghu. 6.21). Another sense is fixity, stability, strength, permanence. 'It is also used in the sense of 'basis, side, foundation, as in ग्रहप्रतिष्ठा. The other sense attached to this word is installation, inauguration.' It also means 'a support' moreover, it means 'fame, senown, glory', e.g. मा निषाद प्रतिष्ठां त्वमगमः The last sense only survives in Hindi while all others have been abandoned.

42. प्रमाण in Kālidāsa means 'a measure', in general. It also means 'testimony, evidence, proof.' In Hindi only the last meaning has been retained, while all the others have been abandoned.

43. प्रसङ्ग in Kālidāsa means 'attachment, devotion', e.g. स्वरूपयोग्येसुरत प्रसङ्गे (Kum. 1.19). It also means 'union, intercourse, association, connection,' e.g. गणिकाप्रसङ्गात् This very sense has been developed in the meaning of 'context' in Hindi.

44. प्रसन्न in CDK means 'pure, clear, bright, transparent.' It also means 'pleased, delightful, propitiated, soothed ?' e.g.

गम्भीरायाः पयसि सरितश्चेतसीव प्रसन्ने (Megh.). Here the word has been used in both the senses. The word also means 'true, correct,' e.g. प्रसन्नस्ते तर्कः (Mal. 1). It is also used in the sense of 'kind, kindly, disposed, gracious, propitious, plain, open, easily, intelligible'. But in Hindi this word is used in the sense of 'pleased, delighted.'

45. बल in Kālidāsa means 'strength, power, might, vigour.' It is also used in the sense of 'an army, host, forces, troops.' In Hindi the word बल is used in the sense of 'strength, power, vigour, might.'

46. भाव in Kālidāsa means 'being, existence.' It also means 'state, condition, e.g. लताभावेन परिणमितमस्या रूपम् (Vik. 4).

It is also used, though very rarely, in the sense of 'idea, thought, opinion, feelings, sentiment,' e.g. एको भावः etc. in Hindi this is used in the last sense.

47. महाजन in CDK means 'a multitude of men, public.' It also means 'the populace, mob.' e.g. महाजनो स्मेरमुखो भविष्यन्ति (Kum. 5.7). It is also used in the sense of 'great man.' It is also used, though very rarely, in the sense of 'the chief of a trade'. This very sense has developed in Hindi in the sense of 'a particular caste of traders in India i.e. Bania'.

48. रुचि in CDK means 'light, lustre, splendour, lightness'. It also means 'ray of light'. Moreover, it means 'appearance colours, beauty'. It is also used in the sense of 'taste, relish, zest, hunger, desire'. Moreover, it is also used in the sense of liking, taste ?' e.g. भिन्नरुचिर्लोकः

Only this last sense has become prominent in Hindi.

49. लांछन in CDK means 'a sign, mark, token'. It also means 'a name, an appellation'. It is also used in the sense of 'a mark of ignomy.' This very sense has developed in Hindi in the sense of blame.

Conclusion

Words of Kālidāsa,—then, change in the course of history, which is why his works often need un-inviting little footnotes.

Geography as well as history plays its part in limiting the meaning of the words of Kālidāsa ; as soon as we try to work with two or more languages semantic problems are multiplied dramatically.

Conclusion

From the above description Kālidāsa's literature can be analysed from two points of view defined by its ontological character. First the author has a reality and he tries to represent an important message of this in the literary texts. The question of how the text information resembles something different, which the text intends to be the representation of—can be called *mimetic* relation. The other possible view is the reader's, with the questions of what the reference of the text to the reader's reality construction, or what type of words can be inferred from the given text for an interpreter. This reference to a world over an interpreter may be called analogical relation. Now the reference mechanism of the works of Kālidāsa may be understood by the following figure :

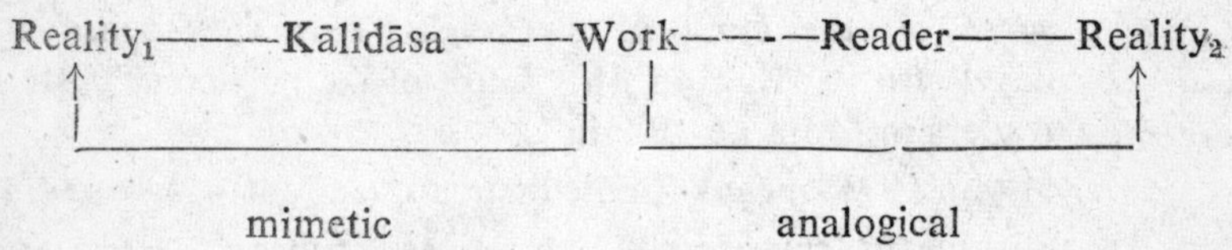

4

STYLISTICS

In the mind of the reader the works of Kālidāsa usually stand as 'an integral whole', and indeed it is profound organic unity for which Kālidāsa always strives. This does not, of course, prevent the sophisticated reader from picking out the various aspects, or component parts of a work of his literature, and all the more aware is Kālidāsa himself of what keeps the plot moving and of the means he uses to bring to life the ideas he has conceived.

The scholarly study of the works of Kālidāsa involves analysis of their structure and evolution of a system of ideas and categories which will characterise the specific traits of the work of literature and of the literary process in general. Obviously these ideas and categories will be of use to us only if they are substantial, if they correspond to the realities of the works in question and help us to understand their structure, development, social and aesthetic experience. This is no less true for the criteria by which we evaluate style.

The complex and changing connections between method and style emerge in a different way in the works of Kālidāsa. What he is showing in his realistic depiction of life is first and foremost the social and political side of his times, with sharp analysis and pertinent ideas diffused with the spirit of criticism. Also characteristic of his work is the large part played by satirical allegory in the Shākuntala and Raghuvansha. Mild satire is the beauty of Shākuntala. In it the human follies and frailities are depicted. In the second Act there is a mild satire of court-life.[1]

1. सेनापति (जनान्तिकम्) सखे: स्थिरप्रतिबद्धो भव । अहं तावत्स्वा-मिनश्चित्तवृत्तिमनुवर्तिष्ये । (प्रकाशम्) प्रलपत्वेष वैधेय: and so on.

There is a satire on polygamy also.[1] In the last chapter of Raghuvansha there is a satire on over indulgence for amours (XII. 34-37, XIX. 7), and so on. This satirical device is very evident in the vocabulary and the structure of the narrative as also in the parodies of bureaucratic circumlocution.

Kālidāsa's style is often explained by the fact that he had to express his ideas and show the reader his understanding of life and attitude. Here also, there seems to be an inner contradiction between Kālidāsa's style and his method, through a close unity of both is inevitably traced. This unusual style is not, however, totally due to the censorship ; for not only does his satirical device veil his ideas and images, but act also directly criticises actual social institutions. Kālidāsa's ideas are simply expressed metaphorically, and it is this which gives its integrity to his Vaidarbhī-style.

There are, of course, not the only examples we could give of differences between style and method. It is something which occurs throughout Sanskrit literature.

Differences between method and style are especially evident when Kālidāsa decides in advance to base his narration on a contrast between the basic tone of the narration and the events and characters described, as in many of the dramatic works. There are other forms of narrative and dramatic actions which display the same differences (Mālavikā. I). But what we have already noted is enough to show that there is no justification for subordinating method to style or for seeing in style the more mirror-image of method.

The most usual explanation is that in his style, Kālidāsa's artistic personality is expressed, along with his overall view of life. It is, of course, true his personality coming out in different ways in his lyrics, epics, and dramas, is especially evident in his style. But a creative personality such as that of Kālidāsa may turn to any number of means of embodying his view of life in artistic images. Thus in Kālidāsa we often find several different styles. After the change in his views, Kālidāsa wrote almost simultaneously the matchless lyric Meghadūta. Still he does not understand how to

---

1. विदूषक :—यदि भवानन्तः पुरकालकूटान्मोक्ष्यसे तदा मां मेघप्रतिच्छन्दे प्रासादे शब्दापय ।

bring love under control and turn into a nobler passion. This knowledge makes Kālidāsa realize that the mission of the life is the service to humanity. He poetises this truth in the Shākuntala. These two styles are as different from each other as both are from Kumārasambhava and Raghuvansha. Kālidāsa had three stories to tell and all the stories were written in different styles.

And if we compare his three dramas written for popular audience, we sec that in his dramas too, Kālidāsa wrote in different styles. Whatever the period and whatever the work, of course, Kālidāsa is still Kālidāsa, and while his style changes from work to work, he had series of stories written in a single style. Fundamentally Kālidāsa was a romantic poet, but he gave romantic expression of Meghadūta to the theme of social inequality in Mālavikā and to heroic poetry in Raghuvansha. With his realism came a new style, characterised by a combination of social protest, satire and the identification of his lyrical self with the fate of his people. And his dramas have a special place in his work, because of the unique way in which they depict the situations that have a decisive influence on the formation of the ancient man.

The change to a new styte is often the result of the writer's artistic evolution and changes in his view of life and artistic method. Along with artist's outlook, the subject itself has an important part to play in the formation of his style and the conflicts that are the moving force behind the work. The specific nature of the problems and questions with which the artist is dealing have an undeniable effect upon the means which he chooses of depicting and expressing them through imagery and style.

In 'Ṛtusaṁhāra' the new subject and new material were 'neutral', until they had gripped the creative imagination of the author in 'Meghadūta'. Once he had entered the sphere of his artistic thinking (through Meghadūta) he had a real effect upon the process of creation. As he studied his raw material from the nature, the writer was obliged to find an adequate means of expressing it in art.

This does not, of course, mean that the appearance of a new raw material in the author's life would call forth the emergence of a new style. Because of differences in the material, the same object affects the author in different ways.

Of even more importance than the raw material of life in the formation of his style is the inner orientation towards the reader which is there, consciously (in dramas) or unconsciously (in lyrics), throughout the process of creation. For the talented artist like Kālidāsa, having his reader in mind does not mean limits imposed upon what he conceives and searches for in his work, but an awareness of the effectiveness at which he aims at. The spiritual contact with his reader is not only the overall aim of Kālidāsa's writings, but also the stimulus to write which has a great effect on the structure of works and their style. Kālidāsa's desire to express the ideas and images that mean much to him is inseparable from his desire to convince the reader of their significance for life and art and to capture the mind of the reader with the structure of his narrative, his lyrical expression and the way he develops the dramatic conflict. His literature has become art because it has the strength to act upon the aesthetic perceptions of the reader. His style is truly all-embracing which enables it to influence very different readers.

As we come to look at poetic language of Kālidāsa, we must first of all note its significance not only as an element of the basis of his literature but also a stylistic phenomenon. As a stylistic phenomenon poetic language of Kālidāsa fulfils a complex role, creating the intonational pattern outside of which not one of the components of style could exist. At one and the same time the poetic language of Kālidāsa is the means of depicting character and as such it is itself to subject to the overall tone and the system of undertones. This inner relationship between the separate word or the verbal texture of each episode of the works of Kālidāsa is the hidden reality in his linguistic style.

The intonational representative and expressive function of the poetic language of Kālidāsa when at one with its communicative qualities gives us a complex and multivalent relationship between the word or the verbal texture of his work and its system of images or structure. On the basis of this emerges the disclosure of the semantic palette of the word, the richness of semantic nuances, changes and contrasts upon which scholars of literary styles are right to lay so much emphasis. It is often remarked that the word lives and plays its part in a particular context or environment. Thus the independence of his poetic language and intonation affects not only the vocabulary, but also the choice of syntactic constructions and the profound relationship between them.

And in the discovery of what old and new in reality, Kālidāsa has at his disposal all the resources of Vedic language, whom I have called "superstratum", an also all the richness of his native language 'Prakrit'. His language is like and ocean with a multitude of hidden currents flowing in and out of one another, and, to a certain extent contradictory one another which make for a vocabulary with a variety of stylistic colouring bearing different relations to the literary norm.

The very nature of Kālidāsa's individual vision of the world, along with the dominant note in his style, dictates his choice of those language forms which will give vivid expression to his artistic concepts. Not only, of course, does he choose his forms but also carries out the complex and deliberate task of organising them. It is because the languages of Kālidāsa are a unified whole and its separate components each of their own task, great or small, to perform that there is no justification on the basis of 'key-words'.

4.1. Superstratum

The forms of the Vedic language which affect the speech of Kālidāsa, remind us that Kālidāsa's language is not absolutely pure, (in the sense of being free from Vedic elements); no matter what purists may say. Vedic superstratum in Kālidāsa may be broadly classified into four heads: Lexical, Semantic, Morphological and Phonological.

In the first instance we have following words taken *verbatim* by the poet from the Vedic texts : रोदसी, सूनृत, अद्धा etc.

It is Kālidāsa in whom we first come across the word रोदसी in the sense of heaven and earth. In the very benedictory verse of Vikramorvashiya the poet says about Shiva :

वेदान्तेषु यमाहुः एकपुरुषं
व्याप्य स्थितं रोदसी ।

Another word used freely by Kālidāsa is सूनृत and it is used in feminine as an epithet of speech: भवतीनां सूनृतयैव गिरा कृतं आतिथेयम् (Shākuntala); सूनुः सूनृतवाक्—(Raghu. 1.93) etc. This is also a Vedicism.

The third word used by Kālidāsa is अद्धा meaning 'truly', (see Raghu. XIII. 65). Though the word is noted in the Amarakosha, it is very rare in classical Sanskrit. Monier Williams thinks it to be a Vedic word.

In some instances semantic change may also be established. Thus the poet says of Sita in the Raghuvansha (XIV. 13): स्वश्रुजनानुष्ठितचारुवेषम् कर्णिरथस्थं रघुवीरपत्नीम्. Mallināatha takes the word कर्णिरथ occurring here to mean 'a small lady's vehicle' (स्त्रीयोग्योऽल्परथ:), but dictionaries do not say of स्त्रीयोग्यत्व. These analyses cannot give satisfactory meaning, unless we know its Vedic derivation कनि, used in the sense of कन्या; like जनि in the sense of जाया. This word कनि compounds with रथ्य to become कर्णिरथ meaning 'a lady's vehicle'.

The instances we have been discussing are all in the realm of lexicology and semasiology. Other alleged instances of superstratum influence involve morphology, as when extension of the verb form आस in place of बभूव. e.g. शेषाङ्गनिर्माणविधौ विधातुर्लावण्य-उत्पाद्य इवास यत्ना : (Kumar. 1.35). आस is an irregular formation from √अस् 'to be' and it can best be explained in the light of Vedic superstratum.

Reference may be made of the word समा used generally in the plural number meaning 'years'. Though used in classical Sanskrit also, it is more frequent in the Vedas. But in Kālidāsa (Raghu. VIII. 24, 92, XIX.4 etc) we find frequent use of this word.

As regards words formed after Vedic models; we have plenty of uses in Kālidāsa. We would like to mention first of all the use of perfect participles. कानच् and क्वसु are sattires used in the Vedas in place of perfect tense. In classical Sanskrit their use is restricted to a few roots and accordingly we get a limited number of forms. It is curious to note that Kālidāsa uses the perfect participle forms as freely and frequently as any classical word. Thus, he not only uses those permissible in classical Sanskrit, e.g. निषेदुषीम्, आसेदुषीम्, उपेयुष:, उपेयिवान्, निषेदुषी निषेदुषा, अनूचान: etc. (Raghu. II, 6,VI. 53,73; XI. 22; XII. I; XV. 83; XIX. 18; Kumar. VI. 15 etc.), but also takes the license of using क्वसु with the other roots like पत्, गम्, स्था etc. (see Raghu. V. 61, XI. 65, 91; Kumar. VI. 64). No other Sanskrit poet than Kālidāsa has used this suffix क्वसु so copiously.

Another peculiarity of the morphological operation noticed in Kālidāsa is violation of Paṇinian rule of अनुप्रयोग; e.g.,

तं पातयाम प्रथमं आस पपात पश्चात् (Raghu. IX 61.)=पातयामास
प्रभ्रंशयं यो नहुषं चकार (Raghu. XIII.36)=प्रभ्रंशयाञ्चकार

and following Vedic one.

It appears in all probability that Kālidāsa followed Vedic pattern in uses of some prefixes. In classical Sanskrit the prefix is immediately followed by the root. No deviation is allowed. But in the Vedas the prefix can follow the verb or can be separated by intervention of any other word or words. Kālidāsa follows the Vedic path.

Vedic substratum is most frequently invoked to explain development in Kālidāsa's phonology. Kālidāsa often shortens vowel for metrical necessity which was originally a Vedic phenomena. Thus we get दूति and दूती in a number of places (Raghu. XVIII. 53, XIX. 18; Vikram. IV. 25; Kumar. IV. 16 etc).

The influence of a substratum becomes perfectly plausible when we find the word त्रियम्बक in place of त्र्यम्बक in Kumārasambhava.

We can therefore easily postulate that Vedic language enjoyed social prestige in the days of Kālidāsa, though it was on the road to extinction. In this connection, it is rewarding to examine the superstratum in Valmik and later classical writers; then only we can postulate any definite theory.

4.2. Prākrita words

The Prakrita words (total number 4040) of Kālidāsa can be divided into three divisions : तत्सम, तद्भव देशी in the traditional way. The last category consists of words not traceable to Sanskrit. An alphabetical list of these words is presented in the III volume of my Dictionary with notes. The term '*desi*' means belonging to the country i.e. provincial or perhaps aboriginal. It is the usual practice of the commentators to designate by this name all the words which they are unable to derive satisfactorily from Sanskrit and considered to have had their origin in the country or of non-Aryan origin. But in reality most of these words can be traced back to Sanskrit with slight phonetic changes such as उल्लाम् which is from आर्द्र. But Ranganāth, the commentator of विक्रमोर्वशीय had stated that it is a *desi* word. Some words like मश्चली and अय्युअ are not included in the list of *desi* words given by Hemachandra and Trivikram. All the desi words may be compared *with the list of the words* given in *Desināmamala*, Pailalacchināmamala and Prākritaśabdānuśāsana. Some of these desi words like अम्म and चिल्ल etc. are of Dravidian origin. It is interesting to note that most of these desi words are retained in New Indo-Aryan languages with certain phonetic changes. Let us take some discussions on the use of Vedic language and Prakrit language in the works of Kālidāsa.

There is no doubt that female characters are realised through their own Prakrit forms ; their choice and deliberate use help to convey what is unique about them as a particular artistic generalisation. Kālidāsa does not, however, create a series of separate characters but a work of unity, in which are revealed not only the consistent ideas underlying it but also the consistency of his poetic language and however specific the language forms used to denote one character or another, we can never say that the languages of the works of Kālidāsa divide into separate units ; it is one and indivisible.

Kālidāsa's choice of Vedic and Prakrit forms and the way in which he organises them are aimed at expressing what is characteristic, fresh or unexpected in the things, feelings and events depicted by him. The distinguishing feature of the Vedic or Prakrit form in the literary usage is that it prompts us to a multitude of thoughts, ideas and explanations.

The potential of the word of depiction in Kālidāsa is at its widest in lyrical which expresses feelings and thoughts. Often the poet feels no need for anything to be depicted openly in order to realise his concept and consequently there is nothing described straight forwardly in his poems. The criteria by which the exactitude and expressiveness of a word are measured are different for the different types of literary style. Here, some of the major points have been analysed.

4.3. The Suggestive Power

Indian literary criticism has always emphasised the suggestive power of Kālidāsa's language, its power to evoke the aesthetic experience called 'Rasa' in the reader or spectator. Thus, Kālidāsa, language is unequalled in its sources of suggestion and is an excellent example of ध्वनि. A quotation from Kālidāsa here would not be inappropriate : it would reveal the suggestiveness:

अनाघ्रातं पुष्पं किसलयमलूनं कररुहै—
रनाविद्धं रत्नं मधु नवमनास्वादितरसम् ।
अखण्डं पुण्यानां फलमिव च तद्रूपमनघं
न जाने भोक्तारं कमिह समुपस्थास्यति विधि: ॥ (Shak.)

The technical perfection of Kālidāsa's verse is something which never ceases to excite the wonder of the reader. Kālidāsa had paid attention not only to parts, but also to the whole, rather a rare thing in Indian poets who generally get lost in details and forget the beauty of the work as a whole. Each verse of Kālidāsa is a product of careful craftmanship. Every epithet is significant. Every verse gives a closure visual picture of what is described. There is no mixture of metaphors. What there is a figure of speech, there is complete symmetry between उपमान and उपमेय. The sounds of each word in a verse are so appropriate that there is a very pleasing flow when one recites the verse.

Kālidāsa tastes poetry as he tastes, for example, a glass of प्रयाणक or शर्बत. He has nothing to do with the character, biography, personal likings and dislikings, peculiar habits or hobbies or range of reading. No Sanskrit critic has ever tried to investigate whether Kālidāsa was polygamous or Bhavabhuti was frustrated in his personal life, or whether there is any historical background behind Raghu's conquest in Kālidāsa's great epic. Nor was a critic only a technician to analyse the lines and words of each stanza to squeeze out all the possible meanings by applying the principles of figures of speech (as this critic claims to do). They rather declared that excellent poetry is possible even without any use of figures of speech, the only source of poetic excellence being a type of suggestive meaning (व्यंजना), other factors enhance its beauty (Sahityadarpana, Chap. I).

Sanskrit critics were to a great extent free from bias because their method was mostly theoretical, that is they referred to individual poets only as examples in analyzing their theories. But this does not mean that they were incapable of criticism of individual poets or this method was unknown to them. Commentators on different works of poets were exercising this method partly because they were not writing directly on authors but they were believing that the picture of an individual poet will automatically emerge out of the anlyses of his different works. Though

Mallinātha did not write a critical book on Kālidāsa, his commentaries on the works of this poet sufficiently make us aware of Kālidāsa's poetic value.

4.4. Word-Order

In Sanskrit, as is known to the students of the language, words can be arranged in any order without incurring any grammatical or semantic lapses. It does not mean that their arrangement involves no artistic acumanship. Kālidāsa being a born artist was fully aware of this fact. He adheres to the stylistic principles as far as the arrangement of words in his works is concerned. Let us cite an example to illustrate this point : The effect of गच्छति पुर: शरीरं धावति पश्चादसंस्तुतं चेत: (Shak. 1.32) artistically weighs much more the line शरीरं पुर: गच्छति धावति पश्चादसंस्तुतं चेत: in which noun and not the verb has been placed first. This is so because in writer's mind what is of paramount significance is the movement of the body and not the body itself. This is missed lamentably when verb is not given the initial position in the poetic utterance under reference.

We may conclude this extremely sketchy discussion, that hardly touches upon all important questions of word order and leaves even many of the discussed problems open, that even in Kālidāsian Sanskrit with so-called free word order, word order is far from being free. This is a fact that can be brought to fore only by means of a more subtle analysis than has been undertaken so far.

4.5. Choice of Metres

The precept that sound 'should echo to the sense' is nowhere better illustrated in Sanskrit literature than in the works of Kālidāsa. A glance at the metres used by the poet is sufficient to prove this. The use of metres like मन्दाक्रान्ता (The whole of Meghadūta is in this metre), हरिणी, वंशस्थविल to portray the sentiment of pathos ; of स्रग्धरा and शार्दूलविक्रीडित to clothe more or less serious thoughts ; of मालिनी and वसन्ततिलका to describe spontaneous feelings, and of आर्या (which is apparently Kālidāsa's favourite metre in dramas) to enunciate simple home-truths would corroborate the truth of the above remark. (R.D. Karmarkar, 1971.135).

उपजाति seems to be Kālidāsa's favourite metre. In a total of 2894 verses in seven works of the poet not less than 856 are in this metre. Kālidāsa considered इन्द्रवज्रा and उपेन्द्रवज्रा as varieties of उपजाति which yields a total of 16 varieties including these two pure metres. If he did not consider these two metres as forms of उपजाति, he would have used only 14 varieties of the mixed metre.

(S.B. Rao, Kālidāsa-Samīksha, 82).

We also notice certain metres being employed usually for certain kind of descriptions. For example, वियोगिनी is used for depicting the behailing of Rati in the fourth canto of Kumārasambhava and of Aja in the eighth canto of Raghuvaṁsha. The metre in Kumārasambhava VIII and in Raghuvaṁsha XIX is रथोद्धता where the subject-matter is dalliance.

It can be concluded that bonds of metre do not chain the poetry of Kālidāsa ; on the other hand they beautified and are beautified by it. क्षेमेन्द्र is right in his statement that even incompetent metres are made competent by a master poet as the undisciplined are disciplined by a powerful leader.

(S.T. III. 10 see V.A. Śarma)

4.6. Un-Paṇinian Usage : Deviation

Kālidāsa shows his knowledge of grammar by using many complex grammatical constructions in his works. In the light of this it should be quite interesting to note the ungrammatical formations that occur in his works. The commentators explain these away by saying that there are आर्ष प्रयोग. The sages and seers are not bound, as ordinary people are, to observe strictly and with meticulous care of the rules of grammar— निरङ्कुशाः कवयः (see M.P. Dwivedi, कालिदास की निरंकुशता)

There are a number of such forms in Kālidāsian works as are not sanctioned by Paṇini's grammar. Are these to be considered as correct ? This is a big question that poses itself to all connoisseurs of old literature. All along the tradition it has been believed that a word may be correct if it has been used by master writers or authorities of language even though it may not be sanctioned by grammar. व्यवहार or usage by eminent writers has been assigned a place even above grammar. This view, however, runs counter to the theory of those who solely rely on Paṇini to decide about the correctness or otherwise of a word (Satya Vrat : The Ramayaṇa—a linguistic study, 1964-173).

Tarapada Chowdhury (Linguistic Abberrations in Kālidāsa's writings, 1-40, 1951) and V. Subba Rao (The un-Paṇinian usages of Kālidāsa, 34-53, कालिदाससमीक्षा, Tirupati, 1962) have analysed in detail the un-Paṇinian usages of Kālidāsa. Prior to these studies, commentaries and दुर्घटवृत्ति (1172 A.D.) dealt with the un-Paṇinian usages. About one hundred such un-Paṇinian usages are found in the works of Kālidāsa. We propose to list all such forms as are recorded in दुर्घटवृत्ति (ed. by Ganapatishastri, Madras). The numbers in brackets refer to the page numbers of दुर्घटवृत्ति.

अनाराध्य Raghu. 1.77 (78)
अपर्णामिति Kum. 5.28 (46)
अवमन्य Kum. 5.33 (113)
आक्रमयामास Kum. 6.52 (29)
आस Kum. 1.35 (56)
आह Raghu. 3.25 (68)
उच्चैस्तराम् Kum. 7.68 (100)
उत्तरेण Megh. (49)
उद्वेजिता Kum. 1.5 (7)
ऐन्द्रम् Raghu. 2.50 (87)
काञ्चनी Megh. (91)
कुशीलवौ Raghu. 15.32 (108)
कृत्रिमपुत्रकैः Kum. 1.29 (100)
केकयीम् Raghu. 13.59 (86)
गिरिशम् Kum. 1.60 (65)
गुरुलाघवम् Shak. (94)
ग्राहयितुम् Kum. 1.52 (29)
ग्रैवेयम् Raghu. 4.75 (88)
चतुर्दिशीशान् Kum. 5.33 (53)
चरन्ति Kum. 3.72 (68)
चुचुम्बे Kum. 3.38 (21)
जातिस्मरौ Raghu. (65)
ज्ञास्यति Kum. 2.31 (68)
ज्योतिष्मती Kum. (96)
त्याजितम् Megh. (29)
त्वगुत्तरासङ्गवतीम् Kum. 5.16 (97)

दधतु: Raghu. 1.26 (15)
दव: Megh. (64)
दृढभक्ति: Megh. (108)
नदीष्ण: Raghu. (65)
नितान्त Kum. 3.4 (113)
निधिर्जलानाम् Raghu. (42)
निविशती Raghu. 12.38 (16)
परीया: Megh. (58)
पाण्ड्या: Raghu. 4.49 (58)
पातयां प्रथममास Raghu. 9.61 (62)
पार्वतीपरमेश्वरौ Raghu. 1.1 (43)
पीतप्रतिबद्धवत्साम् Raghu. 2.1 (79)
पीवरोरु Kum. 8.36 (84)
पुर: कौतुकाधानहेतो: Megh. (30)
प्राक्तनजन्मविद्या: Kum. 1.30 (88)
फलवत्पूगमालिना Raghu. 4.44 (97)
बालाम् Raghu. 6.53 (83)
बिसकिसलयच्छेदपाथेयवन्त: Megh. (97)
बुभुजे Raghu. 15.1 (20)
भवितव्यप्रियसंगमम् Kum. 4.44 (79)
भूषणभूष्यभाव: Kum. 1.42 (43)
मन्दं मन्दम् Megh. (134)
महाँ हि Raghu. 2.56 (138)
रञ्जनात् Raghu. 4.12 (113)
वंशे Megh. (27)
वरम् Megh. (73)
वाम् Raghu. 15.69 (135)
वाहयेत् Megh. (61)
विगाह्य Kum. 1.1 (79)
विनिन्यु: Raghu. 3.29 (18)
विश्राम: Raghu. 1.54 (127)
विषवृक्ष: Kum. (46)
वीज्यते Kum. 2.42 (57)
वैदेहिबन्धो: Raghu. 14.33 (109)
शरीरार्धहराम् Kum. 1.50 (37)

शशिना सह Kum. 4.33 (49)
शार्वरस्य Kum. 8.58 (89)
शिञ्जत् Megh. (14)
शेषम् Kum. 2.44 (71)
सख्याः Megh. (106)
सम्मार्जदक्षा Kum. (128)
सत्रे Raghv. (21)
सहचरीम् Raghu. 9.57 (65)
सितेतरस्य Kum. 1.38 (34)
सुदती Kum. 1.53 (102)
सुभ्रु Kum. 5.43 (23)
सौहृदः Kum. 8.1 (127)
स्मितस्य Kum. (46)
स्यात् Kum. 1.48 (77)
स्वयंग्राह Kum. 3.7 (73)
स्वायम्भुवम् Kum. 2.1 (117)

Narayana Bhatta (1618 A.D.) in his अपाणिनीयप्रमाणता (ed. by Pandit Raman Namatıri, Trivendrum, 1942) also deals with some of the un-Paninian usages. He concludes the book in the following passages :

पाणिन्युक्तं प्रमाणं न तु पुनरपरं चन्द्रभोजादिसूत्रं
केऽप्याहुः तल्लघिष्ठं न खलु बहुविदामस्ति निर्मूलवाक्यम् ।
बह्वङ्गीकारभेदो भवति गुणवशात् पाणिनेः प्राक्कथं वा
पूर्वोक्तं पाणिनिश्चाप्यनुवदति विरोधेऽपि कल्प्यो विकल्पः ।।

4.7. Iteratives

Reduplication of words is one of the expressive devices in Kālidāsian language to convey repeated, intense or continuous action. We can distinguish three types of reduplication in Kālidāsa:

(a) Complete reduplication formed by complete repetition of the first word.

(b) Partial reduplication formed by a part of the word only repeated.

(c) Reduplicatives in which the second word is a debased form or an echo of the first word. (see Chatterji Comm. Vol. of Bharatiya Sahitya, an article on 'iterative Compounds of Kālidāsa, by the present author).

The following is a fairly complete list of iteratives in Kālidāsa. They have been presented here according to parts of speech.

Substantivized iteratives

अर्ध्यमर्ध्यम्, अहन्यहनि, कष्टं-कष्टम्, काले-काले, गृहे-गृहे, दिने-दिने, दिवसे-दिवसे, देशे-देशे, दिशि-दिशि, धनुर्धनुः, निशि-निशि, पदे-पदे, पर्वते-पर्वते, भट्टिनि-भट्टिनि ।

Pronominal iteratives

एष-एषः, कः-कः, तं-तम्, तांस्तान्, तैस्तैः, तेषु-तेषु, यं-यम्, येन-येन, सः सः, स्वेषु-स्वेषु ।

Adjectival iteratives

अल्पाल्प, चकितचकितम्, क्षामक्षाम, दुखदुःखेन, नवोनवः, मन्दं-मन्दम्, मन्दमन्दातपम् ।

Verbal iteratives

जयतु-जयतु, तिष्ठ-तिष्ठ, त्वरस्व-त्वरस्व, पश्य-पश्य, परित्रायतां-परित्रायताम्, पूरय-पूरय, संहर-संहर, समाश्वसितु-समाश्वसितु, समाश्वसिहि-समाश्वसिहि ।

Participal iteratives

खिन्नः-खिन्नः, न भेतव्यं-न भेतव्यम, स्थित्वा-स्थित्वा, स्रस्तं-स्रस्तम् ।

Indeclinable iteratives

आश्चर्यं-आश्चर्यम्, अविहा-अविहा, अलमलम्, इतः-इतः, ईषदीषद्, तत्र-तत्र, ततस्ततः क्व-क्व, न-न, न....न, पुनः-पुनः, भूयोभूयः, न खलु-न खलु, मा-मैवम्, साधु-साधु, यतो-यतः, हन्त-हन्त, हा, धिक्-हा, धिक्, हेले-हेले, रे-रे ।

4.8. Redundant words

The amount of information which is communicated by Kālidāsa over and above the required minimum is redundancy. The language of Kālidāsa utilises redundancy, since much more information is given in normal circumstances than is really necessary to guarantee comprehension. Here are some of the examples of lexical redundancy :

1. गर्भोदराणाम् (गर्भ or उदर)
2. अभ्रघनात् (अभ्र or घन)
3. नाममुद्रा (नाम)
4. अश्वसादिन् (अश्व)
5. अधरोष्ठे (ओष्ठ)
6. कृत्रिमपुत्रक (कृत्रिम)
7. समवस्था (सम्)
8. धनुर्ज्याः (धनुः)
9. कामिजनसार्थः (जन)
10. गीतार्थभावमाकर्ण्य (अर्थम्)
11. कौतुकहस्तसूत्र (हस्तसूत्र)
12. विस्रगन्धी (गन्धी)
13. तालद्रुमवनम् (द्रुम)
14. शिखण्डिबर्ह (बर्ह)
15. जघनकाञ्ची (जघन)

In the above examples, the words in brackets are superfluous items.

4.9. Synonyms

The relationship between name and sense may be of a simple type like one name and one sense. Or, it may be a complex type where more than one name or more than one sense are involved, and in such cases the problem of multiple meaning arises. Multiplicity in form and meaning is common phenomena in the language of Kālidāsa. It arises broadly when : (a) several names are attached to one sense and (b) conversely several senses to one name. A situation of the former type is called synonymy and of the latter type polysemy, which we have already discussed.

Words of different phonemic shapes but of identical or closely similar meanings are called synonyms. They may be interchangeable in any context. Synonymy also is not a phenomenon amenable to a systematic description. It is said that complete synonymy is a rare occurrence and a luxury which language can ill-afford. There are usually minor differences in meaning, usage or feeling—tone between any two synonymic words. It is essential that synonymous words must belong to the same grammatical case.

Some linguists and literary critics think that style is primarily a matter of choice of synonyms and Kālidāsa is expert in choosing the appropriate symbolisation of the experience he wishes to convey among a number of words whose meaning is roughly, but only roughly, the same. The choice of कुमार for स्कन्द, for example, or अटवी for अरण्यम् or विपिनम् would for these linguists and literary critics be a matter of style.

4.10. Polysemy

Polysemy is a normal feature in the semantics of Kālidāsian language. All the "Key words" in addition to their primary meanings acquire one or several additional meanings in different contexts and retain at the same time their previous meanings.

CDK stands testimony to this striking phenomena of words. For example, take the word इति which connotes twenty one different meanings (see 4.2.).

Whatever may be the causes or conditions resulting in the multiplicity of meanings of a word the fact remains that it is a source of ambiguity in Kālidāsian language. This ambiguity of meaning which results from polysemy is removed by contextual situation which alone determines the true import of the word. Grammarians and linguists have generally discussed this problem of ambiguity in relation to polysemy in the language system. Bhartṛhari states that context-grammar is most important factor which enables a language to tolerate polysemy without giving rising to ambiguity.

4.11. Imagery

Imagery plays an important part in the *semantic structure* of the language of Kālidāsa. It makes the poem autonomous and keeps it growing. On this stage, his language becomes more than mere expression and feeling.

It is by his choice and use of images that Kālidāsa is the most remarkable of all the poets of all times. Every word in him as a picture. The unparalleled wealth of his imagery shows itself in that royal use of metaphor which is the most distinguishing quality of his style. Kālidāsa's metaphors stem from the poet's strong and constant impulse to create life or to transfer life from his own *spiset.* His sense-perceptions are the most potent means by which he articulates his spiritual intuitions. The image he creates gives quality and atmosphere and conveys emotion in a way no precise description, however clear and accurate, can possibly do. The fulness of his soul overflows to account for rationally and logically. They stir us because they make our sorrows and desires quiver beneath the music words and the panoply of colours ; their sophistry notwithstanding, they touch and awaken something in us which we call spiritual at the sorts of our being.

Kālidāsa's great novelty lies in the advance that he makes from the purely decorative to the functional image, there is a complete change in the destination of the image. In his poetry, thought and emotion express themselves in terms of images, in a simultaneous mental operation. In fact, he was thinking in images, in order to arouse the emotion more directly in the cource of unfolding and development of the idea. His images came with great spontaneity under the stress of heightened emotion. The great bulk of metaphors and similies are derived from direct observation of the things in nature and in life. The most are largely imaginative and fanciful, by far the greater number being personifications, chiefly of states, qualities and emotions. The Meghadūta is one of the Sanskrits of Kālidāsa's poetic art because we find in it that intimate fusion of human emotion and poetic vision, the superb balance of poetic imagery and the ecstasy of passion which is personal and yet the most universal. His imagery animates the world of the senses apprehended through it and admits infinite variety in quality, intensity, discretion and symbolic function. It seems that in Meghadūta Kālidāsa blossoms forth in all the plentitude of his nature (quoted from Roychoudhuri, IL, XIX.2).

4.12. Idioms

It is generally agreed that the study of idiomaticity in classical languages, specially in Kālidāsian language, is one of the most neglected and under-explored aspects of linguistics. The term idiom has, nevertheless, been around since antiquity and used in a variety of senses, with some more frequently and consistently used than others. Sweet (1889 : 139) observes that "the meaning of each idiom is an isolated fact which cannot be inferred from the meaning of the words of which the idiom is made up."

The idiomatic usage of a linguistic form is one of the most productive forces of motivation in language. If a word or word-combination with conventional meaning is used to suggest a characteristic meaning other than its normal one, we have the idiomatic usage of the expression. Here we impart a special meaning to a familiar word or phrase unpredictable in terms of its structure.

The primary focus of research in the case of Sanskrit idioms is semantic, secondarily lexicographical, and only thirdly syntactical.

The idiom structure of Kālidāsian language can be stated under two broad categories

(i) Phrasal Compound idioms :
(ii) Verb idioms

PHRASAL COMPOUND IDIOMS

The present classification of phrasal compounds may be re-classified under the following three headings :

(*a*) *Compounds with Noun plus Adjective*

आस्थापराङ्मुखः (Raghu. 10.43)
जन्मभीरुः (Raghu. 18.33)
प्रणयमन्थरः (Raghu. 19.21)
विकल्पपराङ्मुखः (Raghu. 17.49)
विचारमूढः (Raghu. 2.47)
श्रवणकटु (Raghu. 6.85)

(*b*) *Compounds with adjective plus noun or adjective plus adjective*

अतिशिथिलसौहार्द Shak. 6
अनन्यदृष्टिः Kum. 5.20
अन्यसंक्रान्तहृदयः Shak. 6
अविरलवाष्पजलाकुलनयनः Vik. 4
आप्तवाक् Raghu. 13.60
आर्द्रमनः Vik. 4
आर्द्रान्तरात्मा Megh. 2.35

नेत्रकौतूहल Megh. 1.51
नेत्रकौमुदी Kum. 5.71
नेत्रविवर Raghu. 9.61
नेत्रनिर्वाणम् Shak. 3
नेत्रोत्सवः Ṛtu. 3.9
पितृगौरव Raghu. 18.39
पुण्डरीकाक्ष Raghu. 10.9
पुण्यगन्ध Raghu. 12.27
पुरुवंशप्रदीप Shak. 1
पुष्करपत्रनेत्र Raghu. 18.30
प्रज्ञाचक्षु Mal. 1
बाणपातपथवर्ती Shak. 1
बिम्बाधर Megh. 2.7
बिम्बाफलाधरोष्ठ Kum. 3.67
भुजबन्धन Kum. 3.39
भुजलता Raghu. 9.46
भ्रूविलास Megh. 2.37
मनःशल्यम् Kum. 2.22
मन्मथेन्धन Raghu. 19.27
मुक्तिमार्ग Kum. 3.5
यशःशरीर Raghu. 2.57
यौवनोष्मा Ṛtu. 5.9
रघुवंशप्रदीप Raghu. 10.68
रतिपण्डित Kum. 4.18
रहस्यदुर्ग Vik. 1
राज्यतृष्णा Raghu. 12.19
लोकयात्रा Mal. 5
लोकशोषण Raghu. 12.29
वागमृत Raghu. 10.48
वाष्पवृष्टि Raghu. 16.44
विरहसमुद्र Vik. 4
विलोचनजल Raghu. 19.56
विषवृक्ष Kum. 2.55
विषादशल्य Shak. 7
शरीरबन्ध Raghu. 13.58

शरीरयष्टि Raghu. 6.65
शोकतम Raghu. 10.2
शोकानल Vik. 4
शोणितमद्यकुल्या Raghu. 7.49
शृंगारदीक्षागुरुः Ṛtu. 6.36
श्रोत्रपेयम् Megh. 1.13
सिद्धिपथ Mal. 1
सुनीतिपादप Mal. 1
सुरतप्रदीप Kum. 1.10
हविर्भुजम् Raghu. 1.56
हस्तनिक्षेप Vik. 5
हस्तावलेप Megh. 1.14
हृदयचोरः Vik. 3
हैयंगवीन Raghu. 1.45

VERB IDIOMS

Verb idioms may be analysed under the following three categories : (I) The human body (II) Life and (III) Emotions.

(I) The Human Body

The Eye etc.

लोचनाभ्यां पिबति Raghu. 2.19; लोचनैः पीयमानः Megh. 1.16; नेत्रैः पपुः Raghu. 2.73; दृष्टिः पिबति Raghu. 13.30
कटाक्षः पतति Vik. 4; चक्षूंषि पतन्ति Shak. 6; नेत्रव्रजाः निपेतुः Raghu. 6.7
चक्षुः ददाति Shak. 1.6; दृष्टिं दाति Mal. 1.2
चक्षुषा पश्यति Raghu 8.78; चक्षुषा पश्यन् Kum. 5.32
विलोचनानि व्यापारयामास Kum. 3.67
लोचने अमिमीत Kum. 5.15
लोचनैः वंचितः Megh. 1.29
लोलापाङ्गैः रमते Megh. 1.29
चक्षुः प्रविशति Raghu. 6.12

The Ear

कर्णं ददाति Shak. 5
कर्णौ पिधाय Shak. 5
कर्णपथं न आयाति Shak. 6

The Lip

अधरं दर्शयति Shak. 7

The Back

आर्द्रपृष्ठाः क्रियन्तां वाजिनः Shak. 1

The Mouth

मुखं पपौ Kum. 8.80
मुखे पतति Shak. 2

The Soul

पात्रीकृतात्मा Raghu. 18.30
अन्तरात्मा प्रसीदति Shak. 7

The Life

जीवितं धारयति Shak. 4
प्राणान् धारयति Raghu. 14.42

धी

धियां पथि वर्तते Kum. 6.22

धीरता

धृतिरस्तमिता Raghu. 8.66

The Youth

यौवनं सन्नद्धम् Shak. 1.20

The Heart

वेपते हृदयम् Shak. 3; Mal 4.5; Vik. 2
आश्वस्तं मे हृदयम् Mal. 5
प्रसीदति मे हृदयम् Mal. 5
प्रेषितं हृदयम् Vik. 2
चोरितं हृदयम् Vik. 3.17
कातरं मे हृदयम् Mal. 3
शङ्कितं मे हृदयम् Mal. 3
हृदयमाचष्टे Mal. 4
हृदयं विदद्रे Raghu. 14.33
हृदयं विश्वसिति Mal. 3
हृदयं भित्वा Vik. 1
हृदयं निवर्तयति Vik. 3
हृदयं संस्पृशति Shak. 4

हृदयानि हरति Ṛtu. 6.24
हृदये करोति Mal. 1
हृदये वसति Kum. 4.9
हृदयशल्य Vik. 1.5

The Mind

प्रोत्कण्ठयति मनः Ṛtu. 3.5
स्निह्यति मनः Shak. 7
प्रकुर्वते मनः Ṛtu. 1.6
दुःखायते मनः Mal. 5
तृप्तं मनः Raghu. 5.11
उद्व्यसितं मनः Kum. 6.14
मनश्चलयति Ṛtu. 3.10
मनो न दूयते Kum. 5.48
मनः द्वैधीभवति Shak. 2.17
मनः करोति Shak. 2
मनस्तु मे संशयमेव गाहते Kum. 5.46
मनांसि मदयति Mal.
मनसि वर्तते Mal. 2
चित्तं हरति Ṛtu. 4.9
चित्तं रमयति Ṛtu. 5.3
चित्तं क्रियते Ṛtu. 1.5
चित्तं विदारयति Ṛtu. 3.6
चेतसा स्मरति Shak. 5
चेतः धावति Shak. 1.32
चेतः दुनोति Kum. 3.28
चेतः व्यथितम् Ṛtu. 6.20
उत्सुकयति चेतः Mal. 5
हरन्ति चेतः Ṛtu. 2.20
प्रहितेन चेतसा Kum. 5.42

4.13. Scientific and Technical Words

Kālidāsa's choice of words is the most important single factor in determining the effectiveness of his writing. Some critics have gone so far as to maintain that effective style is simply the right word in the right place, and they are supported by evidence found in the works of Kālidāsa. The cloud messenger of the Meghadūta of Kālidāsa reveals how carefully he considered each word—writing first one, then another—before finally deciding which was the most likely to convey precisely the effect he intended. The style of Kālidāsa reflects in almost every sentence the search for the *mot Juste*, that one word that can suggest a precise shade of meaning.

Every word of Kālidāsa has its use, and every word has its history. Words of Kālidāsa can be studied from several points of view. We are concerned here with the scientific and technical words of Kālidāsa.

The details mentioned in any description or statement seem extremely natural, though on closer examination one feels that their choice has been influenced by tradition in convention. When he describes the marriage of Shiva and Parvati, the details mentioned may all be found in the Grihyasutras. Certain words are used which reveal his close acquaintance with grammar. Other could have been brought in only by one who knows his Koshas very well. Where he describes the behaviour of kings and ministers, one feels certain that he is thinking of the teachings of Arthashastra. The teachings of Dharmashastra seem to form the background of all his works, whether epic or dramatic. Sometimes the allusions to the systems of philosophy are so specific that only one who had an intimate knowledge of then could have made them. In the VIIth canto of Kumārasaṁbhava, he seems to be perfectly at home with the *Kāmashāstra*. In other words, if one scratches Kālidāsa, one finds scientific and technical knowledge everywhere. But his greatness lies in this that he knew how to hide all this with his poetic genius. It is the poetic beauty of his works which strikes the reader first, the presence of shastra at every step reveals itself only on reflection. Ānandavardhana tells us in *Dhvanyāloka* that gifted poet can hide his deficiency in culture by the brilliance of his poetic genius and quotes Kālidāsa as an example. To me it seems that what Kālidāsa's genius hides is not any deficiency of culture but an abundance of it which in the case of a lesser poet may have managed to smother the poetic quality of his words but which is kept in the background by Kālidāsa's genius. This Kālidāsa has introduced learning into poetry.

4.14. Conclusion

According to Indian critics Kālidāsa was the greatest exponent of the Vaidarbhi style which possessed ten qualities (अर्थव्यक्ति प्रसाद, श्लेष, माधुर्य, सुकुमारता, समता, ओजस्, उदारता, कान्ति and समाधि). His works contain simple words that can be easily found in ordinary lexicons. There are simple compounds, the metres and grammatical constructions are plain. His sentences are pithy and ioconic, but full of meaning. His occasional violations of the rules of Pāṇini are to be taken as deviant method of style. "He is just praised for his happy choice of subjects, his complete attainment of his poetical intentions, for the beauty of his representations, the tenderness of his feeling and the richness of his imagination" (Dr. Bhau Daji's essay on Kālidāsa). Dr. Keith (CSL 46-48) "The Kāvya style unquestionably attains in Kālidāsa its highest pitch, for in his hands the sentiment predominates, which serve to enhance it instead of overwhelming it. Sentiment with him is the soul of the poetry, and fond as he is of the beauty due to the use of figures, he refrains from sacrificing his main purpose in the search for effect. An essential feature of the Vaidarbhi style is the use of pleasing sounds; so that his employment of harsh combinations is censured by Mammaṭa. In the use of Arthālaṅkāras, Kālidāsa is particularly happy and is cited repeatedly as a model by the writers on poetics. His forte is declared to lie in similies, and the praise is well deserved..."

5

THE EVOLUTION OF LITERATURE : KĀLIDĀSA AND HIS READERS

The evolution of literature cannot be divorced from the movement of time, and the two processes interweave on several different planes. Any age of history with the antagonistic elements that co-exist within it will give rise to dissimilar or even totally different literary phenomena. They are the children of their age and reflect this in different ways including that of flatly refusing to depict what is typical of the period. One of the important characteristics of great work of art or literature is that not only do they contain the features of the time which produced them, but they also have a vital effect upon the generations that are to follow.

It is impossible to grasp the nature and the hidden structure of a work of literature without investigating its social origins and its background, and it is because of this that literary criticism lays such stress upon the study of the *work's historical genisis.*

Kālidāsa lived in the times of the famous Gupta kings, a period between 320 and 455 which is generally regarded as India's golden age. In the times of the above mentioned Chandragupta II—perhaps also in Kālidāsa's time—a Chinese Buddhist, Fa Hien, lived for about ten years in the kingdom of the Guptas and left an enthusiastic description of conditions there.

The Gupta Kings ruled over a mighty kingdom which included almost all of northern India, the broad Ganges basin between the Himalayas and the mountains of Deccan, the northern area of which belongs to the West-East Narbadā line. In the mountain Jungles farther south lived mainly tribes of hunters, gatherers and primitive planters still living under practically Stone age conditions (Mālavika was carried off by such robber members of Bastar tribes). In the river valleys and scattered cultivated areas in Southern India, however, there were already artisans working in iron, and there were kingdoms (such as Nala dynasty of Bastar) which could look back on centuries of history. The earliest Aryan settlers of the Ṛgveda soon spread themselves from their north-western home eastward, and mixed racially with the Dravidian and Austro-Asiatic inhabitants of central India, evolving new forms of religion and language.

It seems that from the fourth century onwards feudal ownership of land began to develop. But alongside this, marked elements of old system remained for a long time. Kālidāsa's works confirm this general picture of indigenous and foreign currents.

His poetry is for all times and for all climes beyond the limit of the individual, time and space, revealing the universal truth for common goodwill.

The history of Kālidāsa's literature shows clearly that different ages see with different eyes both the works of Kālidāsa as a whole, and his books taken separately. How different the evaluation of Kālidāsa have been over the centuries ? During the classical period, Kālidāsa was very much liked in India, his lyrics admitted to display all but his dramas did not demonstrate that much fame.

Kālidāsa was discovered in central India in the 473 by Mandasor inscription. Later on he was discovered for the Persians in 531. The Panchatantra translated into Pahelvi for Khusru Anushirvan of Persia (531-579) quotes (1.51) a verse from the Kumārasaṁbhava (11.55), which places Kālidāsa long before 500 A.D. as the Panchatantra must have taken some time to become famous to be translated into a foreign country and the Kumārasaṁbhava, too, must require some time to be quoted as a classical work in Panchatantra.

The Sanskrit poets and critics were ecstatic in their appreciation of Kālidāsa, seeing his work as a model of the extremely bright and daring art, bursting through all the canons and fossilised scholastic rules. He became something of a rallying point for Sanskrit poets in their struggle with classicism and its dogma. This did not, however, prevent Ānandavardhana, Vāgbhaṭa, Kṣhemendra, Amritānanda, Viśwanātha, and Panḍitarāja Jagannāth from being extremely critical in their attitude to Kālidāsa.

The works of this immortal poet and playright won countrywise fame from sixth century to present time. The matchless qualities of his works have been lavishly praised by the poets of seventh century. Dandin (600) compliments Kālidāsa on polishing the Vaidarbha style of composition :

लिप्ता मधुद्रवेणासन्यस्य निर्विषया गिरः ।
तेनेदं वर्त्म वैदर्भं कालिदासेन शोधितम् ।।

(Avanti-Sundari-Katha, Introductory Verse, 15)

Bāṇa (608-648) speaks of him in the following words—"who will not delight at the sight of Kālidāsa's fine sayings like honey-laden shoots, so fresh and sweet" :

निर्गतासु न वा कस्य कालिदासस्य सूक्तिषु ।
प्रीतिर्मधुरसान्द्रासु मंजरीष्विव जायते ।।

(Harshacharita, Introductory Verse, 16),

The work of this poet was also an inspiring example not only for poets and critics, but also for many realist writers. We have only to recall Ravikīrti (634 A.D.) and the extent to which Kālidāsa influenced the formation of inscriptions. Ravikīrti imitated Kālidāsa in the freedom and breadth of his character delineation and the simple spontaneous depiction of his types :

येनायोजि न वेश्म स्थिरमर्थविधौ विवेकिना जिनवेश्म ।
स जयतां रविकीर्तिः कविताश्रितकालिदासभारविकीर्तिः ।।

(Aihole Inscription of Pulakeshina II)

But even in the 8th century when the fame of Kālidāsa as one of the greatest artist of all time was universal and secure,[1] voices of doubt.

Thus, Kālidāsa's work was received in a complex and contradictory way. In its evaluation, there was no unanimity with

1. (a) Kshīraswamin, a commentator on the 'Amarakōsha', has quoted from Kālidāsa.
   (b) In Gauḍavaho, a Prakrit poem of the 8th century, Kālidāsa is referred to as Raghukāra.
   (c) Kumārilabhaṭṭa, the famous Mimaṅsa author of Tantravārtika has quoted Kālidāsa in his work.

its different layers of society, and although his work won recognition and glory very quickly, its true significance remained in a way hidden.

The interest in Kālidāsa expressed in different periods varied greatly. Periods of great enthusiasm for his work alternated with an occasional marked cooling-off by reformists or purists. In spite of this, however, for almost the fifteen centuries Kālidāsa was the centre of an ideological and aesthetic tug-of-war. To the majority of men and women even today, their own essential preoccupations with love, nature, death, and survival with the earth, the stars, the timeless Absolute, in no way differ from Kālidāsa's own ; and Kālidāsa may still command a willing response from sensitive hearts as he did from the post generations in India—Kālidāsa is indisputably the greatest master-mind in Sanskrit poetry. His genius has been recognized in India from very early times.

साकूतमधुरकोकिलविलासिनीकण्ठकूजितप्राये ।
शिक्षासमयेऽपि मुदे रतिलीला कालिदासोक्तिः ।

(गोवर्धनाचार्यः, आर्यासप्तशती 5 : 86)

यस्याश्चोरश्चिकुरनिकरः कर्णपूरो मयूरो
भासो हासः कविकुलगुरुः कालिदासो विलासः ।
हर्षो हर्षो हृदयवसतिः पञ्चबाणस्तु बाणः
केषां नैषा कथय कविताकामिनी कौतुकाय ।।

(जयदेवः, प्रसन्नराघव 1 : 22)

भासो रामिलसोमिलो वररुचिः श्रीसाहसांकः कविः
मेण्ठो भारविकालिदासतरलाः स्कन्धः सुबन्धुश्च यः ।
दण्डी बाणदिवाकरौ गणपतिः कान्तश्च रत्नाकरः
सिद्धा यस्य सरस्वती भगवती के तस्य सर्वेऽपि ते ।।

(राजशेखरः, शार्ङ्गधरपद्धति 188)

माघश्चोरो मयूरो मुरारिपुरपरो सारविद्मः
श्रीहर्षः कालिदासः कविरथ भवभूत्याह्वयो भोजराजः ।
श्रीदण्डी डिण्डिमाख्यः श्रुतिमुकुटगुरुर्भल्लटो भट्टबाणः
ख्याताश्चान्ये सुबन्ध्वादय इह कृतिभिर्विश्वमाह्लादयन्ति ।।

(विश्वगुणादर्शचम्पू 549)

कालिदासगिरां सारं कालिदासः सरस्वती ।
चतुर्मुखोऽथवा साक्षाद्विदुर्नान्ये तु मादृशाः ॥

(मल्लिनाथ)

पुरा कवीनां गणनाप्रसङ्गे कनिष्ठिकाधिष्ठित कालिदासः ।
अद्यापि तत्तुल्यकवेरभावादनामिका सार्थवती बभूव ॥

(unknown)

उपमा कालिदासस्य भारवेरर्थगौरवम् ।
दण्डिनः पदलालित्यं माघे सन्ति त्रयो गुणाः ॥

(unknown)

काव्येषु नाटकं रम्यं तत्रापि च शकुन्तला ।
तत्रापि च चतुर्थोऽङ्कस्तत्र श्लोकचतुष्टयम् ॥

(unknown)

कालिदासकविता नवं वयो माहिषं दधिसशर्करं पयः ।
शारदेन्दुरबला च कोमला स्वर्गसौख्यमुपभुञ्जते नराः ॥

(unknown)

कवयः कालिदासाद्याः कवयो वयमप्यमी ।
पर्वते परमाणौ च पदार्थत्वं प्रतिष्ठितम ॥

(unknown)

कविरमरः कविरचलः कविरभिनन्दश्च कालिदासश्च ।
अन्ये कवयः कवयः कपयश्चापलमात्रं परं दधति ॥

(unknown)

वयमपि कवयः कवयः कवयोऽपि कालिदासाद्याः ।
हृषदो भवन्ति हृषदश्चिन्तामणयोऽपिहा दृषदः ॥

(unknown)

Vallabhadeva (10th century) was the first not only to discover the power and enormous significance of the poet's artistic generalisations, but also to outline the principles of a historical approach to his work. The critic wrote commentaries on the Raghu;

Kumāra, and Megha: Following Vallabha hundreds of critic such as Sthiradeva (11th century), Dakshiṇamūrti (13th century), Pūrṇasaraswati (14th century), Mallinātha (14th century), Parameshwara (15th century), Sanātana Goswāmi (15th century), Charitavardhana (15th century), Lakshmi Niwās (16th century), Bharatamallika (17th century), Mahima Simha Gaṇi (17th century), Sumati-Vijaya (17th century), Vijaya Sūri (17th century), and Kalyāṇamalla (18th century) are the noted critics and commentators of Kālidāsa. Thus, the work of Kālidāsa has come into contact with the most diverse expressions of Sanskrit literature and culture, each time showing itself to be an inexhaustible source of strength. Its influence has been enormous both in time and space.

One of the greatest events of world-wide importance of the eighteenth century was the access of European scholars to Sanskrit Literature. Abraham Roger translated Bhartṛhari's *Shataka* into Dutch as early as 1651. Warren Hastings employed a number of Brāhmans to prepare a digest of Hindu Law and got it translated into English in 1776. Sir William Jones, a cultured man and representative of the enlightened bourgeoisie, took over the post of Judge in the Supreme Court of Bengal in 1783. In 1789, just at the outbreak of French Revolution, Sir William published Kālidāsa's drama 'Shakuntalā' in an English prose translation. He also brought out for the first time a printed edition of the Ṛtusaṁhāra in 1792. Thus, he demonstrated to an astonished Europe that old India has known the drama, the stage play. He called Kālidāsa the Indian Shakespeare—a somewhat lame comparison, nevertheless.

But in 1791, as the Jacobins—the revolutionary democrats—began to extend the revolution against the big land-owners and the big bourgeoisie in France, George *Forster*, the Mainz Jacobin, produced his German prose translation of Jone's English version of 'Shakuntalā'. He sent a copy to Goethe, the renowned German poet, which impressed him to such an extent that he composed a verse in German to extol this wonderful drama. Goethe's epigram may be translated (Walter Ruben : 1957.1) as follows : If in one word of blooms of early and fruits of riper years, of excitement and enchantment I should tell, of fulfilment of content, of Heaven and Earth; Then will I but say Shakuntalā and have said all.

Goethe had the lines printed in the 'Deutsche Monatsschrift' (German Monthly Journal) as early as 1791, and in the following year Herder of Germany and Nicholai Karamazina of Russia set them at the head before the western world.

Herder, the celebrated German poet (Maxmuller, HSL p. 3) observes again in 1798 : "since Sakontala is unfortunately still the only example of India's perfected culture, one lingers with pleasure over it. We must have more Sakontala in the near future, for they are the finest contributions to the cultural history of the peoples."

Only five years later, in 1803, Herder published Forster's translation of the drama again and added a short dedication in which he gave renewed expression to his admiration for Kālidāsa. Friedrich Schlegel came to know Forster's first edition at the Leipzig Fair as soon as it appeared, and he wrote to his brother about this remarkable work. He went later to Paris to learn Sanskrit and thereafter introduced the study of Indology into Germany.

These few facts indicate how right Goethe was when he wrote later : "Recalling the enthusiasm with which we Germans welcomed this translation of Sakontala we can contribute the pleasure it gave us to the prose in which it came to us" (quoted from Ruben, ibid.).

Forster's work had a very considerable influence on the middle-class society of Europe. It stimulated the western scholars to discover the literary heritage of India. Reviewing Sanskrit poetry in general for the *Quarterly Review* of 1831 (Maxmuller, ibid.) Dean Milman admits that "however encumbered with monstrous and extravagant fiction, and a wild and incoherent mythology, it not only excites our interest, but even to European ears may be found to abound in passages rarely perhaps of striking grandeur or energy, but often of the most exquisite delicacy, of the softest tenderness, of infinite variety and gracefulness of fancy, and what may not least surprise our readers, of the purest simplicity." This was at a time when oriental poetry was prescribed in the mass as offering little more than a confusion of florid diction, and turgid and fantastic poetic conceits.

Lenza translated the 'Vikramorvashīya' in Russian in 1833, Bohtling edited 'Shakuntalā' in Russian in 1842, and Friedrich Bollenzena brought out 'Vikramorvashīyam' again in 1846 with Russian translation. Friedrich Rueckert translated the 'Shakuntalā' again in 1855—this time direct from the Sanskrit—but his version was only published in 1867, after his death.

The publication of Heinrich Heine's posthumous work in 1869 brought to light that Heine had noticed something very important about 'Shakuntalā'. In the chapter entitled "Thoughts and Ideas" he wrote : "Goethe made use of Sakontala at the beginning of Faust," here he means that Goethe conceived the idea of the "Vorspiel auf dem Theater" in the Faust from the prologue to 'Shakuntalā.' In Shakuntalā an actor appears first on the stage and speaks a prayer to Shiva, for Indian drama is deeply rooted in the religious ceremony which used to fill several hours of day and night. Then the stage director comes on, calls the leading actress and informs her that Kālidāsa's drama 'Shakuntalā' is to be performed before a cultured audience, so that the actors must do their utmost.

Goethe's prologue takes the following course : the director comes out on the stage with the theatre poet and the comedian and asks both for their help. He is embarrassed, for his public is frighteningly well read. The poet refuses at first to hear anything of the people and thinks only of posterity. The comedian will hear nothing of posterity and want only to amuse contemporaries. The director wants to produce an impressive spectacle : "Plunge into the fullness of life," the comedian advises the poet ; "everybody lives it, but few knew it. And whenever you seize upon it, it is interesting."

The poet speaks of "the urge towards truth and the joy of deceiving." The three thus discourse on the deepest problems of art in Witty dialogue, quite unlike Kālidāsa, who has only followed the old Indian custom in composing a short prologue which introduces the audience to the poet and the title of the play, since there were no theatre programmes. He takes this opportunity to flatter his audience, which was not composed of a crowd of people looking for entertainment, night after night, in professional theatres, as they were accustomed to do in Goethe's Weimar, but of a small group of gentlemen, nobles and Brahmans, higher officials, perhaps a few wealthy merchants, who gathered on some festive occasion in a comparatively small theatre or hall at the King's court to be entertained. The mass of the people did not even understand the language of the play—Sanskrit. Thus the two prologues are very different, indicating two different kinds of society, each with different expectations of the theatre. But we have to thank the Indian poet for inspiring Goethe to this gem of his art.

Goethe also became acquainted with Kālidāsa's lyric poem 'Meghadūta' from H.H. Wilson's translation into English. In 1811

Wilson was appointed first secretary to the newly founded Asiatic Society in Bengal, and in 1813 he published his first work in Calcutta, the text and translation of the "Cloud Messenger." Goethe wrote one of his 'tame epigrams' on this :

> What more pleasant could man wish ?
> Sakontala, Nala, these must one Kiss ;
> And Megha-Duta, the cloud messenger,
> Who would not send him to a soul sister ?
>
> (Ruben, ibid. 4)

In his "Notes to the West-East Divan" he owns that "The first meeting with a work such as this is always an event in our lives." (Winternitz, 1920). But he also criticised Wilson's translation as too smooth and praised "unseen Kosegarten," who had translated a few verses from the original for him, "which assuredly gave quite a different impression" (Ruben, ibid. 4). But in 1826 Wilhelm Von Humboldt praised this poem of old India for its wonderful description of the beginning of the rainy season, when the first clouds come up from the south. Von Humboldt pays his tribute to the great poet as follows : "Kālidāsa, the celebrated author of the Shakuntalā, is a masterly describer of the influence which nature exercises upon the minds of lovers. Tenderness in the expression of feeling and richness of creative fancy have assigned to him his lofty place among the poets of all nations." (Dr. Bhau Daji, the Literary Remains, Calcutta 1887, p. 1).

After C. Schetz published the first prose translation of the Meghadūta in 1859 in Bielefeld, a number of others followed, some of them in verse (the translation of H. von Glasenapp).

In 1827 Wilson's English translation of Kālidāsa's drama "Urvashī won by Valour" and a short summary of his third drama "Mālavikā and Agnimitra" became known in Europe. "Mālavikā and Agnimitra" was first available to educated Germans through A. Weber's excellent German translation in 1856. Since Wilson's time scholars had doubted the genuineness of this drama and had neglected it until this great Berlin Indologist placed it in its proper light. No less a man than Lion Feuchtwanger prepared it for the German stage in 1917 under the title of "The King and the Dancer".

The Urvashī play had been published as early as 1814 by Bollensen in a German translation. Rueckert had only included a few translated verses from Kālidāsa's epic poem "Raghuvaṅsha." A free metric translation of this work into German by A.F. Von Schack appeared in 1890 and in prose by O. Walter in 1914.

Kālidāsa's seventh work "the Kumārasaṁbhava" was translated by Griffith into English in 1879.

Thus, it took over a hundred years for all seven of Kālidāsa's works which have survived to reach the western world.

At the beginning of the 20th century two sharply contrasting attitudes to Kālidāsa came into conflict. One of them was expressed in the declaration made by British authors : "Let us Kick Kālidāsa off the ship of the present." The founder of a new type of literature Rabindranath Tagore, proceeding from a completely different understanding of the development of culture, saw Kālidāsa as "the beginning of all beginnings". Tagore stressed the idea of continuity in the historical movement of culture and the large part to be played by Indian traditions like those of Kālidāsa in formation and development of literature. Tagore not only propogated Kālidāsa's works and expounded their meaning and philosophy, but also wrote a poem in Bengali in praise of the immortal poet-dramatist. An English rendering (N.N. Gupta, The Modern Review, 1932 : 622-23) of the last stanza of the poem is reproduced below :

> Did you not have joy and sorrow,
> Hope and dispair, even like ourselves,
> O immortal poet ? Were not there always ?
> The intrigues of a royal court, the stabbing in the back ?
> Did you never suffer humiliation,
> Affront, distrust, injustice,
> Want, hard and pitiless ? Did you never pass
> A sleepless night of poignant agony ?
> Yet above them all, unconcerned pure,
> Has flowered your poem—a lotus of beauty
> Opening to the sun of Joy. Nowhere
> Does it show any sign of sorrow, affliction, evil times.
> Churning the sea of life you drank the poison,
> The Nectar that arose you gave away.

After the independence, social transformation and the development of a multilingual Indian culture made Kālidāsa the favourite poet of all the peoples in the land. There is no doubt, however, that the socio-aesthetic function of his work is now different from what it was at various periods and for various sectors of society throughout the last fifteen centuries.

5.1. Changing fortune of the work of Kālidāsa

This holds just as true for the changing fortune of the work of Kālidāsa. Important here are not the changes in the way his work was seen but the quality of these changes and the extent of the difference between one view and another.

Noteworthy in this respect are the opinions expressed about the work of Kālidāsa by Monier Williams—"Shakuntala combines the majesty of Homer with the tenderness of virgil, the luxuriance of Ovid and the depth of Shakespeare. And yet it is simple and contains enough to suggest the old Athenian boast of beauty without extravagance" (Levi, 1890). Thus, he places Kālidāsa side by side with the renowned scholars of the world. It would be hard to find anyone nowadays who would agree with this evaluation of Williams. We can not equate Homer with Virgil or Ovid with Shakespeare, or Shakespeare with Kālidāsa. But the heart of the matter is not only in the difference between our attitude to Kālidāsa and that expressed by Williams but in the reasons why in the 19th century Kālidāsa was valued so highly and why our attitude to him is different.

Such differences in evaluation are worthy of note, but they are not the only noteworthy thing to be met as we study Kālidāsa. What is Kālidāsa's place when compared with other established world authors ? Since the (1789) days of William Jones, Kālidāsa has been repeatedly described as the Shakespeare of India. Time has shown that William Jones and his followers were wrong both to praise Shakespeare so highly and to see Kālidāsa's work as something to be compared. The impact of Shakespeare's works has gradually weakened, while Kālidāsa's fame has grown and spread throughout the world. Today we cannot think a better comparison for this study of Kālidāsa than the following Judgement of Christian Lassen (Bhau Daji, ibid.) : "Kālidāsa may be considered as the brightest star in the firmament of Indian artificial poetry. He deserves praise on account of the mastery with which he weilded the language, and the fine sentiment with which he imparts to it a simpler or more artificial form according to the subjects of which he treats without falling into the later hair-splitting and overstepping of the boundaries of good taste : an account of the multifarious of his creations, his ingenious invention and happy choice of subjects ; on account of complete fulfilment of his poetical intentions ; and on account of the beauty of his representations, the tenderness of his feeling and the richness of his imagination."

But here too, we are interested not simply in critic's "mistakes" but in what makes him evaluate a work in the way he does. We should take into consideration the fact that William Jones was far from alone in his great respect for the Sanskrit writer. Sylvain Levi, A.W. Ryder, and Monier Williams were among the many who greeted the works of Kālidāsa with enthusiasm in 19th century. Years later Sylvain Levi (1890 : 4) was to put the following in his "Le theatre Indien" : "The supernatural element which pervades the story threatens to enfeeble the play of human passions and diminish the interest."

At various times and for various reasons there have been all kinds of aberrations : a special attitude to Kālidāsa, unjustified praise of admittedly talented ones and the success of works that are artistically weak. In the 10th century in India, for instance karṇapūra was very popular. *Jayadeva* valued his work much higher than those of Bhāsa and Kālidāsa. The widespread popularity, too, of such untalented writers as Rāmila, Sōmila and Menṭha among their contemporaries in Rājashekhara's time is too well known as a phenomenon to merit more than passing reference. In the same way we can recall many instances of Kālidāsa gaining recognition in the third order.

We must not let this lead us, however, to the conclusion that Kālidāsa's contemporaries or successors are usually wrong in their evaluations of his works. This conclusion is disapproved in the first place by the fact that between the inner energy of a work of Kālidāsa and the aesthetic needs of the time when it appears there is a profound and vital connection. In his works Kālidāsa addresses not abstract readers but people belonging to the Gupta society in which he lives, and he himself is under the irresistible influence of thoughts, feelings and aspirations of his time. This explains the immediate reaction to the works of Kālidāsa by his successors, such as Vāgbhaṭa, Viśwanātha and Panḍitarāja Jagannātha etc. It is a different matter that the aesthetic requirements and the taste of one stage or another in the development of Indians society differ both in their social nature and in their level of sophistication. This, of course, leaves its stamp on the way in which a work of Kālidāsa was received. And we must also take into account the complexity of the relationship between the artistic discovery of Kālidāsa and the way it is 'mastered' by the reader, viewer or listener, between the character of his artistic generalisation and its social and psychological projection.

The way in which the major works of Kālidāsa became part of the culture of the subsequent ages is no less diverse and contradictory a phenomenon. The fate and the socio-aesthetic function of his works often do not correspond to his original intentions and even contradict them completely. It would be of interest to the literary historian to understand clearly just what is in Kālidāsa that is ahead of him, and what in him belongs to a future, which, if he could foresee it, he would have dissociate himself from at once. The very idea of "future" is something broad and undefined. And that is why the destiny of the work of Kālidāsa is so complex and interesting.

There is no doubt that the creative life of Kālidāsa is unique, but it appears that there are certain rules here which cover all cases, rules which have yet to be disclosed by research. "Time sifts literature". This bears directly to Kālidāsa. Not everything that he has written stands the test of time. It is sometimes said that a true work of art is inexhaustible. This is only true in the sense that the significance of its artistic generalisations is not confined to some specific period ; however, the fact that works recognised by many generations as classics cease to exert any aesthetic influence shows that their creative potential has gone out. Naturally, not all their elements cease to function at the same time. A work of art is like a complex system which consists of different layers, fixed in a dynamic relationship. It can preserve its aesthetic integrity even when some of its elements become aesthetically neutral, as can be seen in the fate of the works of Kālidāsa. In Raghuvansha (IX), for instance, much space is devoted to discussion of the future of the caste-system, where he favours the four castes discharging their respective duties, but a Shūdra not allowed to adopt an ascetic life.[1] This is a matter of great concern for Kālidāsa. He attempts to revive the caste-system on a new basis. It is natural that contemporary reader should find little of interest in this theme, but

1. तस्मै द्विजेतरतपस्विसुतं स्खलद्भिः (Raghu., IX: 76).

because he is bound up in the heroes, their sufferings and their dramas, these scenes whose aesthetic tension is 'weaker' or which have become emotionally neutral, do not detract from general impression left by the epic or from its impact.

In this case what we are faced with is not the damping down of the work's creative potential but seeing it from a new angle. Even when we meet this aesthetic " neutralisation" we should use caution before speaking of the exhaustion of its inner energy and of the final test of time. The different evaluations of Kālidāsa by different ages and his different evaluations in different countries or even in different provinces of our country are not simply a result of some inner quality which he possesses. These differences are a result of the interaction of his poetic content with the demands and requirements of different readers.

5.2. Socio-aesthetic function

Relationship between Kālidāsa and his readers

Every reader perceives the works of Kālidāsa in his own particular way, and yet definite groups of readers (Indologists) have something in common in their approach to these works. Shākuntala created in a particular period and under particular circumstances, bear the stamp of the Gupta age which gave her birth. But she contains human qualities which belong equally to completely different stages in the development of Indian society and is, therefore, constantly renewed and revitalised. When she enters the life of a different age she is invested with new meaning, and it is this meaning which makes for the multivalence by which she is distinguished.

As we study the active life of the works of Kālidāsa we are bound to take into account all the different ways in which they might be interpreted. Studies containing an account of the changing fortunes of various words have been with us for quite long time ; they became markedly more obscene at the beginning of 12th century. A descriptive note on such tabu words is presented here.

Sixteen years ago, when, I was teaching Kumārasaṁbhava in B.A. (final), at Govt. College Sioni, I avoided to explain certain words of Kālidāsa before the students in the class-room. One day a student of South India rose up from his seat and asked the meanings of those words. It turned out that the avoided words were those which bore some phonetic similarity to the "four-letter" words of Hindi; but they were not pejorative in Telugu. This is why the South Indian student emphasized to know their meanings.

These words are still avoided even though it is doubtful that a Hindi-speaking person not knowing Sanskrit (Kālidāsian language) would, when overhearing Sanskrit utterances delivered at a normal rate of speed for that language, be likely to catch these words and attach any special significance to them. For one thing, not understanding the language, he would be unlikely to concentrate sufficiently to notice the rather rare sequences of sounds which might cause him to think he was hearing Hindi obscene words.

How then did the Kālidāsian taboo develop ? It may be suggested that it arose as a direct result of bilingualism among the Sanskritists. The more Indian languages they knew and used, the more conscious they would be of the phonetic similarity between certain Sanskrit (Kālidāsian) syllables and the taboo words of other Indian languages. Thus, the avoidance (of some of the Kālidāsian words grew as bilingualism increased among the Sanskritists studying Kālidāsa and as they came more and more to think in terms of the modern Indian's taboos.

This tendency of avoiding some of the Sanskrit words of Kālidāsa is not a new phenomena. It prevailed in the 14th century also. We may very much establish on the authority of Viśwanāth that Kālidāsian words, such as लिङ्ग, चूत, विष्टित and वमन were thought to be vulgar in his time hence avoided: चूतविष्टितवमनशब्दा अश्लीला: (साहित्यदर्पण, p. 473) ।

वाग्भट in his काव्यानुशासन (p.28) quotes the following lines of Kālidāsa stating that the word मध्यमणि is vulgar :

तस्या: प्रविष्टा नतनाभिरन्ध्रं...
तन्मेखलामध्यमणेरिवार्चि: ।
अत्र मध्यमणिशब्देनाश्लीलं व्यंज्यते ।

अलंकारसंग्रह of *Amritānanda* (ed. Krishnamacharya, Madras, 1949) censures the use of the word कटि also: कटिशब्दोऽत्र गुह्याङ्ग-वाचकत्वेन गर्ह्यते ।

The syntactic and semantic vulgarity of Kālidāsa has been the subject of discussion since Anandavardhana, when he categorically remarked in his ध्वन्यालोक ।

"तस्मादभिनेयार्थेऽनभिनेयार्थे वा काव्ये
यदुत्तमप्रकृते राजादेरुत्तमप्रकृतिभिर्नायिका-
भिः सह ग्राम्यसम्भोगवर्णनं तत्पित्रोः
सम्भोगवर्णनमिव सुतरामसभ्यम् ।
तथैवोत्तमदेवतादिविषयम्" ।

Kṣhemendra is also critical. He quotes the following verse of Kālidāsa and comments on it in the following manner :

ऊरुमूलनखमार्गराजिभिस्तत्क्षणं हृतविलोचनो हरिः ।
× × × ×
"अत्राम्बिकासम्भोगवर्णने पामरनारीसमुचित-
निर्लज्जसज्जनस्वराजिविराजितोरुमूलहृत-
विलोचनत्वं त्रिलोचनस्य भगवतस्त्रिजगद्-
गुरोर्यदुक्तं तेनानौचित्यमेव परं प्रबन्धार्थः
पुष्णाति" ।

Panḍitarāja Jagannātha also accuses Kālidāsa on his description of dalliance of Shiva-Parvati.

Among the words (of Kālidāsa) pointed out as being avoidable among the different mother-tongue-speakers of India are the following:

1. अण्ड (ज) (=अण्डकोश=testicles)
   निष्कम्पवृक्षं निभृतद्विरेफं
   मूकाण्डजं शान्तमृगप्रचारकम् । (Kum. 3.42)
2. अर्थी (Hindi=corpse)
   गुर्वर्थमर्थी श्रुतपादृश्वा
   रघोः सकाशादनवाप्य कामम् (Raghu. 5.24)
3. इन्द्रिय (Hindi=penis)
   तयोर्यथाप्रार्थितमिन्द्रियार्थान् (Raghu. 14.25)
4. उद्गार (MIA=vomitting) Kum. 1.33.
5. उपस्थित (MIA=penis) Ragu. 8.76
6. कर्बुर (Hindi बुर=Vagina)
   भस्मकपोतकर्बुरम् Kum. 4.27
7. क्लिन्न (रक्तासक्त)

8. गण्ड (anus) Megh.

9. घर्षित (बलात्कार=rape)

10. चूत (Hindi=vagina)
    चूतप्रवालोष्ठम् (Kum. 3.30)
    चूतम् (Kum. 3.30)
    चूतयष्टि: (Kum. 6.2)
    चूतांकुरास्वादकषायकण्ठ: (Kum. 3.32)
    चूते (Kum. 1.27)
    चूतप्रसवम् (Shak. 6.40.3)
    चूतकुसुमम् (Raghu. 19.43)

11. चोद (Hindi=to capulate)
    चोदयामास (Raghu. 4.24)

12. जीमूत (Hindi मूत=urine)
    जीमूतेन (Megh. 1.4)

13. पाद (Hindi=अपानवायु)
    पादान् Raghu. 1.57

14. पित्त (Telugu=अपानवायु)
    विदूषक—भवति त्वरयास्य भोजनं यत्पित्तोपशमन-
    समर्थं भवति (Vik. 2.189)

15. पेलव (Awadhi, Begheli=to capulate)
    पेलवपुष्पपत्रिण: Kum. 4.29

16. बाल (Bengali=hair of private parts)
    बालकुन्दानुविद्धम् (Megh. 2.2)

17. यंत्रित (OIA=सम्भोगबद्ध)

18. वराङ्गनां (OIA=Vagina) Ṛtu. 2.5.4

19. वर्चस् (OIA=Semen)

20. वान्त (Bagheli=Vomitting; Telugu=vomitting)
    वान्तवृष्टि: (Megh.)

21. विष्टा (OIA=latrine)
    नाभिप्रविष्टाभरण (Kum. 7.60)

22. शष्प (Telugu=hairs of private parts) शष्पश्यामान् (Megh.)

23. सम्भोग (sexual union)
    सम्भोगान्ते (Megh.)

24. स्खलित (वीर्यक्षरण)
संसर्पन्त्याः स्खलितसुभगं
दर्शितावर्तनाभेः (Megh.)
25. सुभग (OIA=vagina) Megh.
26. लिङ्ग (Hindi, Telugu etc.=penis)
यतिपार्थिवलिङ्गधारिणौ (Raghu. 8.16)

Mono-syllabic taboo words in Kālidāsa are very rare. Hence the words given here contain more than one syllable.

Now it is apparent that non-Hindi speakers studying Kālidāsa tend to avoid certain words of their own language which bear a phonetic resemblance to Hindi obscene words. Here again they avoid the words only when Hindi-speakers are about, but the reason for the avoidance appears to stem from their own uncertainty about the propriety of using the words because of their knowledge of Hindi. Thus, the tradition of avoidance is a continuous one. The students of Kālidāsa teach each succeeding group of new students about the taboo, and on this way the avoidance is kept alive from year to year and ages to ages.

Thus, the relationship between the words and culture of Kālidāsa can be approached on the aesthetic ground. What we have dealt with is primarily the way in which the classical notions were rejected in the course of time, and the direct effect of the words upon today's reader. It is obvious that socio-aesthetic function of the literature of Kālidāsa is becoming distinct and separate in our age.

5.3. Kālidāsa Contemporary

Throughout the period of 1500 years the Indian people have not changed much in contrast to the living conditions in which they exist. The moral principles of Kālidāsa remain unchanged and so does the moral values of the masses. And this is the reason for our strong links with Kālidāsa, the surprising similarity of contemporaneity with the age of antiquity. This can also be illustrated with some of the sayings of Kālidāsa that we can see the direct relationship between the world of Kālidāsa and our own. The essence of such opinion is that we find ideas in the works of Kālidāsa that are close to some present-day philosophical trend. This is why we see a true connection between the classic and the present day.

All that is best in Kālidāsa is widely recognised and appreciated throughout our society. Dissatisfaction among the readers arises when Kālidāsa does not engage with important problems in the life of society, the development of the individual and his inner world. We could name not a single literary work which was enormously popular for such a long period of 1500 years. There is something very extraordinary in Kālidāsa, who paced with the development of reader's need.

EPILOGUE

Kālidāsa and the Continuity of history

Kālidāsa wrote greatly under the influence of the feudalism that was developing in India in the middle and in the second half of the 4th century, while at the same time his work was in itself one of the essential moving forces of this feudal mentality. He was instrumental in forming the ethical consciousness, helping to the struggle against social evil. This effect was in no way diminished by the writer's own political outlook (Raghu. 4.83 ; 8.4). Kālidāsa was an aristocrat by breeding and a moderate by conviction and that with his sensitive and loving heart he sympathised with and even served the case of feudality.

Kālidāsa's world of poetic images and their objective meaning is, as we have already noted, infinitely broader and more diverse than the political convictions to which he subscribed.

Kālidāsa was a writer of social and psychological dynamism. The main criteria by which Kālidāsa judged the individual's aspirations were his attitude to the interests of society, his devotion to 'Dharma', his spiritual honesty and part played by man in eradication of jealousy, hatred, wickedness, and evil. He inherited and openly subscribed to the 'dharma' that constitutes the human personality. Kālidāsa's heroes and heroines are deliberately selected to represent the godly specimens of humanity so that they might serve as models of conduct. They accept life with all its sufferings keeping the goal of final emancipation in view. Thus he was interested first of all in the inner make-up of the individual and the relationship between his character and the influence on it of the world around him, like the policemen in Shākuntala, he leaves us in no doubt about the empire of evil in the material world.

Kālidāsa became a mature artist and true master of his craft at the end of 4th century A.D., when he completed Shākuntala, where evil appears throughout the work, and he depicts sharp conflicts within the life of society.

Keith (The Sanskrit Drama, p.160) once wrote that these are no great crimes in the work of Kālidāsa, nor will you find there any scene of tragedy. This is also not true. Kālidāsa truly representing the Indian epic tradition has not forgotten to emphasize this, and his heroines Urvaśī and Shakuntalā suffered because of pervasive fate in spite of their innocence. The theme of fate and its vicissitudes interested Kālidāsa even when he left the field of historical events and depicted everyday life instead.

Indian literary critics have done almost no work on the connection between Kālidāsa and Indian literature, a subject that would be of a great and topical interest. Among the authors who have been fruitfully influenced by Kālidāsa we would cite hundreds of examples (see Chapter 5). The part played by Kālidāsa's tradition and those of other great Indian writers in the development of Indian literature is an important subject which has yet to be finally exhausted.

Kālidāsa was the first important Indian author to be widely acclaimed abroad. His works were the first to give foreign readers a broad picture of Indian culture and to bring Sanskrit letters to the forefront of world literature. Kālidāsa's world fame was based first and foremost on what was inherent in his artistic personality, and on originality to his artistic generalisations.

It often happens that a work which throws light upon some deep and complex human problems becomes particulary beloved of young people without losing its attraction for the adult reader as well. Something similar seems to have happened with the work of Kālidāsa, for it becomes increasingly popular with the young people. This is to a great degree because Kālidāsa wrote so vividly and inspiredly about young people and their desire to find their true calling in life. Older and younger readers, of course, see Kālidāsa's work in somewhat different ways, and it is different things in it which attract them. From this view we can conclude that different generations are influenced differently by a work of art not only in succeeding periods of time, but also when these generations co-exist in one and the same time.

There is nothing to surprise us in the fact that this is so even when we hark back to A.W. Ryder's ideas of Kālidāsa as "No other poet in any land has sung of happy love between Man and Woman as Kālidāsa sang". Of itself, artistic perfection and the writer's craftmanship which have affected other writers so profoundly could never be an obstacle to the special interest shown in Kālidāsa's work by young people.

Kālidāsa's outstanding works map out the continuity of history, a happy fate which they share with the greatest works of other distinguished writers.

Kālidāsa and the Experience of Love

Meghadūta is among Kālidāsa's highest achievements. Like Ṛtusaṁhāre, it is quiet, lucid, conventional, and yet deeply personal, an expression of doctrines not merely known, but lived and felt. The more intimately one becomes acquainted with the poem, however, the more puzzling it becomes : and as the climax of the Alkā, a vision of soul's entrance into heaven, it is remarkably untriumphant, unapocalyptic, unvisionary. It discloses the peculiar nature of an extremely compact symbolic narrative that although unusual, is both consistent and satisfyingly complete. Kālidāsa's most admirable qualities as a poet are frequently attributed to the tension in his verse between the public and the private, the universal and the individual, between an inherited system of doctrines and the souls private responses to experience that one affirms its individuality and the universality. Aesthetically, it is also a fitting conclusion to the drama of spiritual anguish, anger, pathos, joy, and despair that has been recorded in the Meghadūta. Its simplicity of idiom declares its sublime resolution of worldly vicissitudes into the transcendent, wordless peace of love's realm.

Women in Kālidāsa's Plays

Kālidāsa's plays show the diversity of the mind of a 4th century man whose understanding of the human condition is extended beyond his own sex and beyond his own time. Because he is genius, because he could hear the words of women and transform them into language on the stage, because he did not filter these words through the screen of contemporary male prejudices, he was able to present vibrant, alive women. Shakuntalā's uniqueness lies in its portrait of a young girl who remains strong during her swift growth to womanhood. It is not proper to regard women in Kālidāsa's plays as less than whole, less than characters whose dramatic stature must be examined from their own vantage point and in their own right.

The Privileged Playgoes of Kālidāsa

Assumptions about the nature of Kālidāsa's audience go hand in hand with ideas about the quality, scope, and even meaning of his dramas. When Kālidāsa was viewed as unpolished genius in British period, his audience were equally primitive in their responses. After independence Kālidāsa thrives in the same milieu as any living great dramatist of India, even then the matter of Kālidāsa's audience is a problem in economics, demographics, and social practices.

BIBLIOGRAPHY

Kālidāsa—Lexicon, Vol. I, Pt. I-III. ed. by A. Sharpe, Brugge, 1958

The Mālavikāgnimitra. ed. by K.P. Parab, Bombay, 1935.

The Vikramōrvashīya. ed. by H.D. Velankar, New Delhi, 1965.

The Abhijñāna-Shākuntala. ed. by S.K. Belvalkar, New Delhi, 1965.

The Raghuvaṅsha. ed. by W.L. Pansikar, Bombay, 1916.

The Kumārasaṁbhava. ed. by W.L. Pansikar, Bombay, 1927.

The Ṛtusaṁhāra. ed. by V.R. Nerurkar, Bombay, 1966.

The Mēghadūta. ed. by S.K. De, New Delhi, 1957.

INDEX